Mark McGuinness is a p clients all over the world author of the Amazon Creativity bestseller *Resilience: Facing Down Rejection and Criticism on the Road to Success*, and a co-author of the 99U bestsellers *Manage Your Day-to-Day*, and *Maximize Your Potential.*

"Mark McGuinness is a rare cat—part poet, part coach for creative professionals, part old-time, overeducated Brit who thinks deeply about stuff you and I have never heard of. His extraordinary new book *Motivation for Creative People* is a deep, unsentimental dive into the quotidian realities of the artist's life—how to stay sane, pay the rent, refrain from murdering your spouse, all while pursuing your calling with purity of heart and nobility of intention. This is a How To manual at the highest level from a man who has lived the life and has watched and worked intimately with hundreds of others who've done the same. Indispensable reading for anyone in a creative field who is seeking to achieve not just a flash of brilliance but a lifelong career."
Steven Pressfield, bestselling author of *The War of Art*

"*Motivation for Creative People* is chock full of stories and tips, carrots and prods. It will give you the kick in the seat of the pants you need to get down to the business of creating. An enjoyable read!"
Roger von Oech, author of *A Whack on the Side of the Head: How You Can Be More Creative* **and the** *Creative Whack Pack*

"When we speak of motivation, we typically refer to some vague combination of inspiration and willpower. In this book, Mark goes much deeper, articulating the complex array of values, rewards, and influences that drive us to make our best work. (Or keep us from it.) *Motivation for Creative People* will encourage you reflect sincerely on the factors that underpin your artistic achievements, giving you a 'clarity of mission' that will take your creativity to new heights."
Jocelyn Glei, author and Founding Editor, 99U

motivation

for creative people

HOW TO STAY CREATIVE
WHILE GAINING MONEY, FAME, AND REPUTATION

BY MARK MCGUINNESS

LATERAL ACTION BOOKS

MOTIVATION FOR CREATIVE PEOPLE

How to stay creative while gaining money, fame, and reputation

ISBN: 9780957566446

Published by Lateral Action Books 2015

LateralAction.com

To Mami, Kano, and Issa—my best motivations

Contents

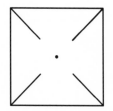

GETTING STARTED

12

CHAPTER 1

Beyond working for love

"I love my work so much I would do it for free."

Many creative people have uttered these words in a moment of enthusiasm—they express the joy of creative work, and the fact that it often feels more like play than work. They also hint at some of the pitfalls that lie in wait for creatives.

In one sense, creative people have no problem at all with motivation. We fall in love with our creative work, usually early in life, and pursue a career path that allows us to do what we love every day.

We work long, hard, and late through choice, because we enjoy it and we want the end result to be amazing. We don't need anyone to tell us what to do, let alone to "motivate" us.

We obsess over tiny details most people would never notice, because "good enough" is not good enough for us—we want the work to be the best it can possibly be.

We have a low boredom threshold, so we are constantly seeking out new challenges. We want to keep stretching ourselves, to keep testing our limits, because that's where the magic happens.

We have a deep urge to follow our dreams, wherever they lead. We want to emulate our creative heroes. To create something extraordinary. To surprise ourselves and astound the world.

Some days we have to pinch ourselves, we feel so lucky that the work that feels like play is our work. Yet the idea that we love our work so much we'd do it for free has a sting in its tail...

HOW MOTIVATION AFFECTS YOUR CREATIVITY

Our instinct to work for love rather than money is backed up by a lot of research into the psychology of creativity. The researchers tell us that we are at our most creative when we are driven by **intrinsic motivation**—i.e. working for the sheer joy of it, regardless of rewards. Focusing on **extrinsic motivation**—such as money, fame, or other rewards—can be a creativity killer.

So if you don't feel excited by the task in front of you, it's impossible to do your most creative and original work, however much money you are offered, or however much pressure you are under—from your boss, your client, your audience, or yourself.

True artists have always known that the quality of their work depends, in some mysterious way, on the quality of their intention: if we are in this for the money, or the fame, or the awards, the Muse will wrinkle her nose and pass us by. Only when we are truly dedicated to the art itself, *for its own sake*, will she bestow the gift of inspiration.

Or to put it more prosaically: only when we truly love our work will we put in the time, and take the care, to do it to the best of our ability. To keep learning and refining our skills all our lives. To first master our craft and then elevate it to the level of art.

BUT CREATIVE PROFESSIONALS CAN'T IGNORE REWARDS

Have another look at these words: "I love my work so much I would do it for free."

We don't say, "I *will* do it for free," but, "I *would* do it for free." The "would" implies "in an ideal world," or "if I didn't have to earn a living." But we do not live in an ideal world.

Working for love is all well and good, but if you are a creative *professional*—meaning you aspire to create work to a professional standard, and/or earn your living from your creativity—there is always something at stake beyond the work itself. Here are three of the big ones:

Money

If your creative work is your main occupation, you can't ignore money. You need to be paid—and paid well, if you want to live well. If you're doing high quality work, you're creating a lot of value, so why *shouldn't* you reap the rewards? To do this, you need to find a way to resolve the "creativity versus money" dilemma.

Fame

Part of the pleasure of creating something amazing is sharing it with other people and experiencing their delight in your work—whether a live audience, enthusiastic customers and collectors, or legions of followers online. It's not just a matter of ego: in some creative industries—such as film, music, literature, and drama—fame is essential to earning a living, since your income is proportional to the number of tickets, downloads, or copies you sell.

Reputation

Sometimes called "artistic reputation" or "critical reputation," this is similar to fame, in that it is about others' perceptions of you. The difference is that fame is about the number of people who know about you, regardless of their opinion of your work; reputation is about how your work is perceived by industry thought leaders (practitioners, critics, connoisseurs, and enthusiasts) and involves a value judgment. It's possible to be very famous with a low artistic reputation, and vice versa. For some creators, especially in the fine arts, reputation is even more desirable than fame or money.

If you are serious about pursuing a creative career—whether in the arts, commercial creativity, or as an entrepreneur—you cannot succeed without pursuing rewards.

You need money to pay the bills, fund your projects, and take care of yourself and your family. In many fields you may not need to be famous, but you do need a good reputation within your professional network. And if you're in a fame-driven industry, you *need* a powerful public profile, whether or not you enjoy the limelight.

But in the pursuit of these rewards you encounter a number of threats to your creativity, motivation, and resilience:

Selling yourself short

Some creatives try to ignore money: they fail to promote their work, shy away from "money conversations," and accept low fees out of fear. But if you sell yourself short, you end up working long hours for little money; you are constantly tired, overworked, and stressed about money. Not only that, but you can feel resentment towards your clients and customers, which makes it impossible to do your best work for them.

Selling out

The opposite of ignoring money is focusing on it too much. You embrace money, celebrity, and the trappings of success, but lose your creative soul. Even if this pays off financially, you cannot feel fulfilled without creating great work. Inevitably, your artistic reputation will suffer. You might think "that would be a nice problem to have,"—but having coached creatives who have lost their way in the maze of success, I can assure you it's not a good place to be.

The weight of expectation

When lots of people are watching you, and there's a lot riding on the outcome, it's hard to do something for the sheer joy of it. The weight of expectation can be experienced directly, in the presence of a live audience; indirectly, via the media and social media; or via money, in the form of high fees, advances, or royalty checks. For performers, this can cause stage fright. For creators it can lead to procrastination and creative blocks.

Comparisonitis

Another way to block your creativity is to look at the achievements of your peers, or the biggest names in your field, or your creative heroes—and compare yourself unfavorably to them. When you look at the fame, fortune, and reputation they have amassed, you feel inadequate, intimidated, and creatively paralyzed.

Professional jealousy

This is similar to comparisonitis in that it involves focusing on your peers and the big names. But instead of thinking, "I'll never be as good as them," you think, "I'm better than them! Why are they getting all the recognition?" In this scenario, you are paralyzed by jealousy and resentment rather than fear, but the effect on your creativity is just as deadly.

Discouragement

It's essential that you create for the love of it first and foremost, and that you learn to validate your own efforts. But you're only human. Your enthusiasm and determination can sustain you for years with little or no reward or recognition for your efforts. But the longer you go without external validation—in the form of money, fame, reputation, and/or opportunity—the more discouraged you can feel, and the harder it is to keep going.

All of these obstacles are a threat to your creativity for the same reason: they take your attention and intention away from the work itself, and towards rewards—or the lack of them. You focus less and less on the work, more and more on yourself, and the work suffers.

It's impossible to achieve your professional ambitions without pursuing rewards. But focusing on rewards can kill your creativity.

It's enough to mess with anyone's mind.

THE DRAWBACKS OF BEING DIFFERENT

When you pursue a creative career, you often feel alone.

The work itself may require long periods of solitude, scratching at a canvas, tapping at a keyboard, hammering metal, carving wood, memorizing lines, or practicing melodies. Even if you are in the public eye or on stage and surrounded by people, the place in the spotlight can feel very lonely. And the more original your career path, the fewer fellow travelers you will have for company and support.

Sometimes it feels like you're on your own, swimming against the tide of conventional wisdom. If you follow your heart, people around you don't "get" your priorities, and pressure you to conform. Yet if you try to suppress your desires and follow the crowd, you can find yourself creatively blocked, depressed, and even ill.

Staying creative over the long term requires both self-knowledge and finding the right people to encourage and support you on your journey.

YOU ARE NOT ALONE

If you struggle with any of these challenges—creating for love versus pursuing rewards, or following your heart versus following the crowd—I can assure you that you are not alone.

I've encountered them myself in my own work as a poet, author, and coach (and previously as a psychotherapist, and a freelance writer/editor). I've also heard about them over and over again, from the hundreds of creative professionals I've coached over the past twenty years.

So if you're facing them too, it does *not* necessarily mean you have a psychological problem. In my experience they are normal occupational hazards for creative professionals.

I have written this book to help you overcome these challenges. It's based on my experience of coaching creative people like you to achieve their ambitions—in their creative work, careers, and/ or businesses.

Sometimes I draw on research from the psychology of creativity, which I studied for my Master's degree. But this book is not based on theory: reading the research helped me to clarify some of the issues my clients and I have faced, but my starting point has been what they, and I, have found practically useful. All the solutions offered in the book have been tested with real people facing real challenges.

The title *Motivation for Creative People* has two meanings. Firstly, it is a book *about* motivation *for* creative people—a guide to different types of motivation and how they affect your creativity and your career. Secondly, it is designed to be a *source* of motivation for you, via stories, new perspectives, and practical tools to equip you for the challenges that lie ahead.

In the following pages I will show you ways to:

- stay creative and in love with your work—even under pressure
- overcome Resistance to tackling your creative challenges
- reclaim your creative soul if you wander off your true path
- stop selling yourself short—and start reaping the rewards of your creativity
- attract the right kind of audience for your work
- cultivate an outstanding artistic reputation
- avoid destroying your creativity by becoming too attached to money, fame, reputation, and other rewards
- surround yourself with people who support your creative ambitions
- avoid getting stuck in unhealthy comparisonitis or professional jealousy
- balance your inspiration, ambition, desires, and influences in the big picture of your creative career

CHAPTER 2

What gets you out of bed in the morning?

It is five o'clock on an English morning in the middle of January, in the heart of the Victorian age. An old man is climbing the stairs, lit by a candle on the tray in his hands. The tray also holds a pot of coffee and a china cup. When he reaches the top of the stairs, he pauses for breath and rests the tray on a small table. Straightening, he knocks three times on the bedroom door, picks up the tray, and enters.

As he approaches the bed, he can make out a head with an enormous beard spilling over the blanket. The master blinks owlishly as his servant approaches, places the candle on the bedside table, and proceeds to pour the coffee.

The beard belongs to Anthony Trollope, the acclaimed novelist, who will author 47 novels in his lifetime, as well as several travel books and numerous short stories. This would be an impressive output for any writer, yet most of these works were written while Trollope was engaged in a distinguished full-time career in the Post Office. Hence the early mornings, as described in his autobiography:

> It was my practice to be at my table every morning at 5.30 a.m.;
> and it was also my practice to allow myself no mercy. An old
> groom, whose business it was to call me, and to whom I paid £5

a year extra for the duty, allowed himself no mercy. During all those years at Waltham Cross he was never once late with the coffee which it was his duty to bring me. I do not know that I ought not to feel that I owe more to him than to any one else for the success I have had. By beginning at that hour I could complete my literary work before I dressed for breakfast.

| Anthony Trollope, *An Autobiography*, 1883

What went through Trollope's mind as he lay there in bed, hearing the knock at the door and watching his manservant pour the coffee each morning? How did he feel? What made him get out of bed instead of turning over for another forty winks?

Was he thinking of the joy of creation, of his characters and the next chapter in their story? Did he bound out of bed, eager to put pen to paper and lose himself in his imagination? Maybe. It's hard to imagine anyone writing 47 novels without taking some pleasure in the process. He must surely have loved writing to dedicate so much of his life to it. I would guess that once seated at his desk, he was soon absorbed in the pleasure of writing for its own sake—otherwise known as **intrinsic motivation**. But was he joyful as he lay there, acutely aware of the contrast between the warm bed and the cold January air? I'm not so sure.

Was he thinking of the money he would make from his books? When *An Autobiography* was published after his death, some of Trollope's readers were shocked at his frank admission that he wrote for cash:

I am well aware that there are many who think that an author in his authorship should not regard money—nor a painter, or sculptor, or composer in his art... But it is a mistake to suppose that a man is a better man because he despises money... Who does not desire to be hospitable to friends, generous to the poor, liberal to all, munificent to his children and to be himself free from the carking fear which poverty creates?

He had actually worked out how many words per hour he needed to write in order to publish enough books to meet his financial goals. His reputation suffered when critics condemned him for such base **extrinsic motivation**. Again, we know that financial reward was a large factor in Trollope's resolve to get up so early each morning. But as he lay there in bed, poised between sleeping and waking, did gold coins dance before his eyes and lure him to the table? Maybe.

Was he simply a very disciplined man, focused on his desire for achievement and made of sterner stuff than ordinary mortals? If so, allowing himself "no mercy" would simply lie in his character and values—his **personal motivation**. But in that case, why would he need someone else to bring his coffee and get him out of bed? Surely he'd trust himself to get up on his own?

Imagine for a moment that you are the great man, lying in that bed. It's nice and warm. You're sleepy. As you poke your hand out from the covers, you can feel the frost in the air. You'd like nothing more than to roll over and go back to sleep. But what would you say to the servant?

"Sorry, it's too cold today."

"I'm tired."

"Can I just have five more minutes?"

Or even worse, suppose you woke up later to find you had nodded off in front of him... Imagine the loss of face!

You're awake now, bolt upright, assuming the mantle of head of the household. In a moment you're out of bed and into character, slipping into the dressing gown he holds for you, thanking him for the coffee, making small talk about the weather and the fireplace. A few short steps and you're ensconced at your writing table, haloed by candlelight. As the manservant leaves the room, you feel a twinge of gratitude, even of solidarity, and appreciation of the effectiveness of this kind of **social motivation**.

Or maybe it was just the coffee.

Trollope's story gives us our first creative motivation principle: **motivation for creative work is complex.**

Different types of motivation interlock and support each other, playing different roles at different stages of the creative process. Yes, Trollope wanted to make money, but his chosen path to riches must have been influenced by a love of reading and telling stories. He must have been disciplined and ambitious to plan such a punishing schedule for himself, yet he clearly did not trust himself to stick to it alone. So he set a motivational trap for himself, baiting it with his vanity—at the crucial moment, he knew he could not stay in bed without humiliating himself in front of his social inferior. No wonder he was so ready to acknowledge the old man's contribution to his success.

We can picture the relationships between the four main types of motivation as a pinwheel:

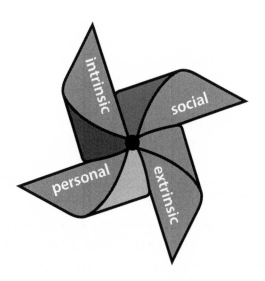

We are used to seeing the blades on opposing sides (intrinsic / extrinsic, personal / social) in terms of conflict or dilemma. We feel we have to choose between working for love or for money; or between following our heart or giving in to pressure from other people.

But if we look at the big picture, we can see that a key to Trollope's success was his ability to strike a creative balance between the different types of motivation: instead of seeing money as the enemy of creativity, he used it to support himself and achieve his ambitions. Although he followed his own inclination to write, he wasn't too proud to ask for help from others. As the wheel turned, it not only powered his writing, it propelled him to success.

The creative process in Trollope's bedroom was pretty straight-forward: the production work only involved two people, although publishers, readers, and the rest of the literary world came into play further down the line. Yet even in his simple creative system we can see the four fundamental types of motivation at work. How much more complex, then, are the motivations, drives, and influences at play in the 21st century creative economy? Today's writers still sit at their desks and write—but their writing apparatus is connected to a global network that would boggle the mind of a Victorian Post Office worker.

Like Trollope, I'm writing this book alone in my office. Unlike him, I have to endure the hardship of making my own coffee. And I have a lot more temptation at my fingertips than he did—with a click of the mouse I could be catching up on my email, scrolling through my Twitter feed, or kidding myself that I'm doing "research" by browsing books on Amazon. In some ways, it's harder for me to stick to my intention of writing a book. On the other hand, I have the luxury of staying in bed till 7 a.m. (kids permitting) and switching on the central heating in winter.

Like Trollope, I'm writing because I **love** to write. The hours I spend writing each morning are a form of meditation—they both center me and take me far away from my everyday life. A day without writing feels like a wasted day.

Like Trollope, I'm aware of the potential **rewards** for writing—money, fame, reputation, new opportunities—but which I must banish from my mind when I start writing each morning.

Like Trollope, I identify as a writer. It's who I am, and what I do. Creativity is one of my deepest **values**. Once upon a time I tried ignoring the urge to create, and it literally made me ill.

But I'm not doing this alone, even though there is no one actually in the room as I write these words. For starters, you are in my mind. We've never met, but we've already spent a few minutes in each other's company. I've spent hundreds of hours imagining you—my ideal reader, someone on the creative path and looking for help—as I write. This book was conceived and written in order to help you. Once I've done my bit, I can say I've "finished" the book, but it's not really finished unless you read it.

And the writer-reader relationship is just one of the **influences** on this book. Another, more immediate influence is the fact that I've promised the manuscript to my editor, David Colin Carr, and I know he has a busy schedule, which gives me another little incentive to finish the draft. Once the book is finished, I will need to find ways of getting it into the hands of readers.

Whatever your creative profession, you will probably recognize a similar mix of motivations for your work: love, money, fame, personal drive, and the influences of others. Depending on the nature of your work and the size of your organization, you may well have a far more complex network of relationships and influences to navigate than I do. If you sometimes feel that reconciling all these motivations and influences is an impossible task, I can assure you you're not alone! But it can be done, and this book will show you how.

My goal is to help you—like Trollope, like me, like the legions of others who devote their working lives to creating something extraordinary—get out of bed and *look forward* to your day's work, for the rest of your days.

CHAPTER 3

What exactly is motivation?

"Motivation" is often spoken of as if it were some mysterious psychological quality that we either possess or do not. Even worse, a supposed lack of it is often used as an excuse for avoiding difficult tasks ("I don't have enough motivation to do that") or as a form of pseudo-psychological diagnosis ("He suffers from low motivation") that is disempowering and—ironically—demotivating to those on the receiving end.

So let's be clear what I mean by the word "motivation" in this book.

It's not a psychological quality inside you.

It's not a personality trait.

It's not something you can put into someone else, by "motivating" them.

So what is it?

The word motivation comes from Old French and Latin roots meaning "to move," "to set in motion."

Motivation is whatever gets you moving.

And not just moving, but full of energy and excitement. Willing to push through the obstacles that stand in your way.

Motivation takes many forms . . .

Sometimes it is a feeling—the simple pleasure of performing a task (such as writing, dancing, painting, or playing music).

Sometimes it is the thought of a reward—whether tangible (such as money and awards) or intangible (such as praise or fame).

Sometimes it is a value or principle that matters to you personally—such as truth, justice, compassion, pleasure, or beauty.

Sometimes it is the influence of people around you—whether directly (in what they say or do) or indirectly (in what you imagine they might say, do, or think).

Often it is a combination of two or more different types of motivation.

THE CREATIVE MOTIVATION PINWHEEL

The relationships between different types of motivation are illustrated in the **Creative Motivation Pinwheel**. The pinwheel embodies the principles of creative motivation in several ways...

It has four separate blades, corresponding to the four basic types of motivation:

1. **Intrinsic motivation**—the joy of work
2. **Extrinsic motivation**—rewards for work
3. **Personal motivation**—your values
4. **Social motivation**—influences from other people

The four blades can be painted different colors, but they are actually made from a single sheet of paper cut and folded, suggesting that the types represent different aspects of motivation, rather than completely separate drives.

The pinwheel spins either when you blow on it, or when a breeze plays on it. Similarly, sometimes it feels like motivation springs from your own desire or discipline; yet at other times, it is as if you are inspired by something bigger than yourself.

When the pinwheel spins, the effect is magical: the blades and colors blur and seem to fuse together. The movement is effortless, beautiful, and delightful.

Movement. Energy. Delight. That's how it feels when all your motivations combine in your work, your career, and your life.

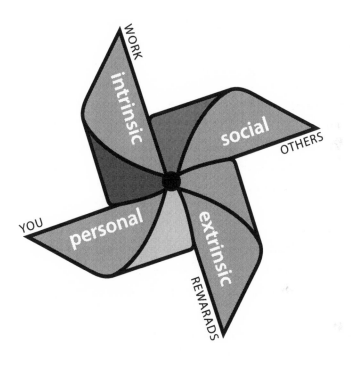

CREATIVE MOTIVATION PINWHEEL

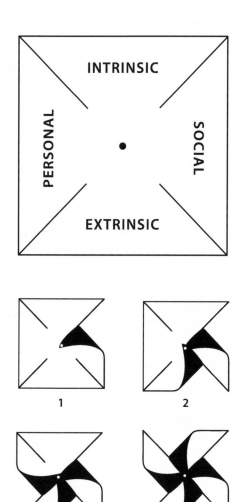

A PINWHEEL: FOUR BLADES FROM ONE SHEET

An impossible dream?

Some people will tell you "You can't have it all," and it's selfish, greedy, or unrealistic to try. They will argue that life and work are hard enough, without expecting them to bring you fulfillment as well as a pay packet. It's a persuasive argument, and you can find plenty of evidence to back it up if you look around you.

It's hard to explain the magic of a spinning pinwheel to someone who has never seen it. If all you have before you is a blank sheet of paper and some scissors, the spinning wheel of rainbow colors is difficult to picture. But that doesn't mean it's impossible, with a little know-how, creativity, and willingness to experiment.

The promise of the pinwheel is to get you out of black-and-white thinking. It's not a case of creativity *versus* money, or following your heart *versus* following the crowd. It's about how to incorporate all four types of motivation in your career, and make them fuse together with joy.

GETTING STARTED

CHAPTER 4

How to use this book

This book is an invitation to stop the world and get off for a little while, to get some clarity on what you really want from your work and life, and to make some well-considered decisions about your future path.

In the next four sections of the book I will examine each of the four types of motivation in turn. I will describe each motivation, the different forms it can take, and how it can affect you and your creativity. Then I will offer some practical suggestions for making the most of it and avoiding the common pitfalls.

Once we've examined the four motivations, we will look at how you can combine them effectively:
- in each project you undertake
- in the big picture of your career.

I'll show you different ways to combine them, and give you examples of contemporary creative professionals who exemplify different combinations—in the arts, in commercial creativity, and in business.

As you'll see from the examples of creators throughout the book, there are many different creative professional paths, and many different ways to combine the different motivations in a creative career. Yet we all experience the same unforgettable joy when we align our desires, ambitions, values, and influences, to set the pinwheel spinning.

At a first reading, you may want to skip or skim the activities, then return to them once the big picture is clear. Whether you do this, or complete the activities as you work through the book, make sure you test the ideas in your own life—by taking action.

Like a coaching conversation, the value of this book does not lie in what is said, or even what you understand, but in *what you do as a result*. Remember, motivation is whatever gets you moving—so get moving!

INTRINSIC MOTIVATION
The Joy of Work

INTRINSIC MOTIVATION

CHAPTER 5

The joy of work

"Let right deeds be
Thy motive, not the fruit which comes from them."
| Krishna, *The Bhaghavad Gita* (translation Edwin Arnold)   37

"Work is more fun than fun."
| Noel Coward

Years ago I was sitting at the kitchen table in my flat on a summer's day, trying to write poetry. Failing to write poetry. It felt like I'd been sitting there for eternity, with nothing to show for it but a pile of scratched out drafts.

Looking at the sunshine outside, listening to the shrieks of children from the park, I sighed and wondered: "Why do I do this?"

The next moment, I considered this thought with curiosity: "Why *do* I do this?"

I realized I hadn't thought about this for a long time. Poetry was just something I did. Or rather, something I wanted to do but mostly didn't. It was more of a source of suffering than satisfaction in my life. So why *did* I bother?

I started to consider the potential rewards of writing poetry. Each time I thought of a reward, my Inner Grouch gave me a piece of his mind in return.

"Fame?"

"Get real. How famous do poets get these days? How many

people could name three so-called famous modern poets?"

"Reputation?" I glanced at the ranks of great poets on my bookshelves. "Earning a place with them?"

"It's hardly a safe bet, is it? Even if you ever produce something half-decent, poets go in and out of fashion like hemlines. What about Samuel Johnson's Lives of the Poets? Nobody these days has heard of most of them."

"Money?"

"I won't even dignify that with an answer."

"So why am I doing this? How the hell did I end up doing something so futile?"

The Grouch went quiet.

Then I remembered a day at school as a teenager. Our English teacher, Geoff Reilly, had set us the task of writing a ballad in response to a novel we were reading. By the end of the lesson my poem was well under way, and I was annoyed when the bell interrupted and we had to troop off to Chemistry. I went to the back of the lab, pulled out my notepad and kept scribbling away at the poem, leaving the Bunsen burner for my lab partner to deal with.

All the way through Chemistry, History, and Geography I kept working at the ballad—or rather, it kept working at me, as if a mischievous goblin had got into the words and made them dance at the corner of my eye, drawing me away from school and deeper into the poem. The rhythm set the words bouncing along, the rhymes falling into place and conjuring new words to fill the next line, and the line after that. I was entranced.

That day I realized I had fallen in love with poetry, because it was far more fascinating, enchanting, and plain fun than any other kind of writing.

That memory silenced the Grouch.

Since that day in the flat, whenever I feel discouraged about my writing, I only have to remember writing the ballad at school and sanity is restored: it reminds me of the goblin in the words, and the altered state I enter when I'm deep into a poem. Then I have all the rewards I need, right there in the moment.

I have a similar feeling about coaching: when I'm deep in conversation with a client, we enter a timeless place where we can stop the world and create something extraordinary together. I also discovered this fairly early on, when I started practicing psychotherapy in my twenties and realized I loved working with people and helping them change their lives.

So now I wake up every morning *looking forward* to my work: whatever else is going on in my life and whatever the ups and downs of running my own business, I know that a day spent writing and coaching is a day well spent. It brings me the kind of satisfaction that goes way beyond any money I earn or recognition I gain.

If you're reading this, I'll bet you feel the same way about your creative work—whether it's your day job or business, or something you pursue in your own time. Early in life you had an experience like mine—you fell in love with your work and you've never entirely fallen out of it, even though there may have been disagreements or trial separations along the way.

Maybe you take this for granted, but in a lot of places the idea of *enjoying* your work would be seen as pretty weird. You'd be regarded as mad or sucking up to the boss. When I worked in a factory it was taken for granted that we all hated being there. No one started work until the buzzer rang. Machines were switched off a minute before it rang for breaks, so that you weren't shutting down in a few precious seconds of your own time. The only possible reason you could have for working late was that you were a "grabber" who wanted extra money from overtime. At the end of the day, some people literally ran out the front door.

But companies that depend on their workers' creativity tend to be different. People want to work there—not just to be there enjoying the trappings and rewards, but to *work* there. When I coach clients in creative companies, I hear complaints about people—colleagues, clients, bosses, etc.—and about systems and processes. But hardly ever about the work itself—unless it's not challenging, difficult, interesting, or plain good enough.

I call this **the Joy of Work.** Psychologists call it **intrinsic motivation**—doing something for its own sake; as opposed to **extrinsic motivation**—doing something in order to gain a reward or avoid a punishment. The good news is that this joy is not just a nice side-effect, but an *essential characteristic* of high level creative work.

WHAT DOES RESEARCH TELL US ABOUT MOTIVATION AND CREATIVITY?

Many research studies have investigated the effect of different types of motivation on creativity. Here are three examples, described by one of the most prominent researchers, Teresa Amabile, in her book *Creativity in Context.*

In one experiment, performed with variations by different researchers, two groups of children were given some pens and paper and invited to draw pictures. One group was told to have fun and draw whatever they liked, while the other was promised a reward—such as playing with a toy—if their pictures were judged to be good enough. The first group, who were drawing for sheer pleasure (intrinsic motivation), were judged to produce more creative and original drawings than the second group, who were drawing in order to impress the grown ups and gain a reward (extrinsic motivation).

In another study, three groups of experienced creative writers, all adults, were asked to first write a haiku poem about snow and then one about laughter. Before writing the second poem, one group was asked to consider a list of "reasons for writing"—all extrinsic motivations, such as impressing teachers, public recognition, and securing a good job—and rank the reasons in order. Another group was asked to consider a list of intrinsic motivations—including pleasure, insight, and self-expression. The third group was a control. Even though the extrinsic group were not offered any kind of reward for their performance, only to consider the relative importance of different rewards, this shift of focus had a dramatic effect on their creativity: their poems about laughter were judged to be much less creative than either their own poems about snow, or the other two groups' poems about laughter.

A third project involved analysis of the works of professional artists. The works were divided into two categories: self-generated pieces, and pieces commissioned by others. When a panel of art experts considered the works, they judged the self-generated works to be typically more creative and original than the commissions. The researchers concluded that this was because the self-generated works were produced from intrinsic motivation, whereas commissions were more likely to be influenced by extrinsic motivations, such as the judgment of the commissioner.

From these and other experiments, Amabile concluded that intrinsic motivation is strongly linked with creativity, while extrinsic motivation is likely to inhibit or even kill creativity.

In other words, *you do your most creative work when you do it for love.*

If you, like me, are something of a Romantic when it comes to creativity, this is good news. It confirms our intuition that creation is an act of love. Our best work is produced in a timeless state where we are totally absorbed in the work itself, with no thought or expectation of reward. You can't buy creativity.

...you do your most creative work when you do it for love.

WHY DOES INTRINSIC MOTIVATION LEAD TO CREATIVITY?

Researchers, careful to avoid rushing to conclusions, have suggested several reasons why intrinsic motivation is linked with creativity, and why extrinsic motivation can inhibit creativity.[1]

a) Completing a task in order to gain a reward transforms it from creative play into uninspiring work.

b) Dividing your attention between the task and an anticipated reward means you are bringing less of your mental bandwidth to bear on the task.

c) Focusing on a reward can make you too eager to complete a task, so that you miss potentially creative alternatives.

d) Working to please a judge or to sell to a market involves setting aside your own instincts and trying to second-guess others' expectations, leading to less original work.

e) If you are more concerned with the reward than the work itself, you are likely to give up when things become difficult, meaning the less easy, less obvious solutions will be out of your reach.

If we flip these round, we can see that:

a) When you do something that feels like play, you want to keep doing it; the more you play, the better you become.

b) When you give something your undivided attention, you put your heart and soul into it and bring your full abilities to bear on it.

INTRINSIC MOTIVATION

---

1 For an in-depth account of research into the effect of intrinsic and extrinsic motivations on creativity, read Teresa Amabile's book *Creativity in Context* (Westview Press, 1996). Another good book, summarizing the research and considering the implications for the way we work, is *Drive: The Surprising Truth About What Motivates Us* by Daniel H. Pink (Canongate Books, 2011).

c) When you are focused on the task itself, you take time to get to know it deeply, exploring many different options, which can lead to surprising discoveries.

d) When you follow your own instincts rather than trying to please others, you are more likely to create something original.

e) When you love the work so much that you persist in spite of difficulties, you have more chance of making an unusual discovery.

Or, to look at it in a different way. If you were the Muse listening to two artists implore your divine assistance to transform their works-in-progress into works of genius, and if you noticed one of them was looking over your shoulder, with one eye on the market, on his professional status, on money, fame, fandom, and the next opportunity, and if you saw the other gazing at her creations with love, bringing all her passion, patience, and persistence to bear on them—whom would you choose to favor?

CHAPTER 6

Types of intrinsic motivation

Just as the ancient Greeks spoke of four types of love, so we can identify different types of intrinsic motivation, which are present to a greater or lesser degree depending on the person and type of work. Read through the types and see which are most important to you.

- **Freedom**
- **Challenge**
- **Learning**
- **Purpose**
- **Inspiration**
- **Creative flow**
- **Obsession**

Freedom

Creators hate being told what to do. In agencies, one of the most common complaints among junior creatives is that the senior people take all the interesting creative decisions, leaving them with the task of executing the routine work. To an extent this is inevitable: every commercial project comes with constraints, every agency has its own style and standards, and it can take a while for even very talented creatives to reach the required standard. Yet in some companies, even experienced creatives are expected to "color within the lines" drawn by the creative director.

When I coach creative directors and managers about this issue, they usually acknowledge it, but have not always grasped how deeply demotivating it can be for team members to have their creative freedom so restricted. These leaders are often pleasantly surprised to discover what a motivational shot in the arm it can be when they allow creatives even a little more creative freedom, on selected projects. Many times I have heard creative directors tell me that it results in incredible levels of dedication, with people working evenings and weekends without being asked, because they are so fired up by the opportunity to exercise their skills and judgment to the full.

Personally, I'm not good at following orders. So for almost all of my career I have been self-employed, either running my own company or as a joint owner with partners. I have gone through a ridiculous amount of stress to preserve this status.

When it came to publishing my books, I was offered several deals from publishers on both sides of the Atlantic, and it was tempting to get their help and associate my name with a well-known brand. But in the end, I decided to turn down the offers and publish the books myself. This was partly a financial decision—it's no secret that you can earn more from a book you publish yourself than if you sign with a publisher. But it was also about creative freedom.

I spoke to some great editors, and there was a lot that was attractive about working with them. But at the point where they started telling me how long the book should be, and that they would be in charge of the title and cover design, I started wondering, "Whose book is this?" The answer, of course, was that if I signed my rights away, the book would no longer be mine. I would lose the freedom to make it as long or short as I wanted, to have the final say in editorial decisions, to choose the cover designer and the cover design, to set the book's price, and to decide how to market it.

Publishing the books myself is more work, and more expensive: I need to hire an editor, proofreader, designer, and formatter, and manage the whole process myself. When I started there was a very steep learning curve, and I have to keep educating myself about publishing as well as developing as a writer. But it's well worth the extra effort for the sheer fun of creating my own book, and seeing it with the title and cover I chose. Each time I look at one of my books, I have the satisfaction of knowing I did it *my* way. I know they aren't perfect, but all the mistakes are down to me, not someone else—and that is priceless.

You probably feel the same way about your projects: the ones that give you the most satisfaction are the ones where you had the most freedom in your creative process and control over the final product.

Challenge

On a hot evening last September I was sitting six rows from the front of the Hammersmith Apollo with my wife and my friend Peleg. Miraculously, Peleg had beaten the stampede to book tickets for one of Kate Bush's first live shows in 35 years.

We were mesmerized: once I acclimatized to seeing Kate Bush a few feet away from me, I realized this was probably the best gig I would ever see. It wasn't just the amazing band and the fact her voice was pitch-perfect; there was a heartfelt intensity to her singing that is impossible to put into words. And the fact she had chosen a tiny, intimate venue like the Apollo felt like a gift. *It doesn't get any better than this*, I thought. Then the world turned upside-down.

As "King of the Mountain" drew to a close, one of the band strode to the front of the stage, swinging a bullroarer. Strobe lighting intensified the effect of the noise, and we were engulfed in a storm of confetti. That signaled the beginning of a phantasmagoric journey through Kate's masterpiece, the "Ninth Wave" sequence from *Hounds of Love*.

As the band played, images appeared on giant screens, skeletal fish creatures scuttled through the theater aisles, over the stage, and back again. A house floated across the stage, with people watching TV and eating dinner on the sofa. I think there was a lighthouse at one point. We felt the rush of air from a helicopter's blades as it hovered above our heads. I have a memory of Kate being carried off stage by the fish creatures in a funeral procession. The combination of music, film, theater, and special effects was so immersive that there were a couple of moments when I "came to" as if I'd just woken from a dream, then remembered with a start I was at a concert.

By the time the curtain came down at the end of "The Morning Fog," we were on our feet and there were people in tears all around us. I couldn't believe what I'd just experienced, and thanked my lucky stars. Then Kate smiled and said, "Thank you very much. We're going to take a break now, then we'll be back for the second half."

The second half?!!

She had already obliterated our expectations. If she'd done nothing else, we'd have gone home more than happy. But there was more . . . and the second half was just as unforgettable as the first.

There was no need for the show to be as good as it was. Bush could have satisfied her fans and critics with far less. But not herself.

Creators love to challenge themselves. The greater the artist, the bigger the challenge they pick. What could be more exciting than doing something as difficult, risky, and unexpected as possible? No wonder Yeats described the compulsion to write poetry as "the fascination of what's difficult."

Watch the documentary *Jiro Dreams of Sushi* and you will see a master chef in his eighties, the owner of one of the most respected sushi restaurants in Tokyo, who has built his reputation through a relentless drive to keep improving his art. Critics queue up to praise Jiro's food, there are no more Michelin stars left for him to collect, and his two sons are experienced chefs in their own right who could run the business for him if he wanted. After years of dedication, Jiro could afford to retire and bask in his achievements. But he keeps working at his craft, constantly innovating with ingredients and preparation techniques. The challenge drives him on.

One thing I've noticed while coaching successful creatives is that while everyone around them is full of praise for their accomplishments, they instinctively look to the future and their next challenge. This kind of ambition can be exhausting—and some of them come to me to learn to take better care of themselves on the journey. But it's also exhilarating to know that you will never run out of challenges as long as you are the one responsible for raising the bar.

Learning

"I am always doing that which I cannot do, in order to learn how to do it."
Pablo Picasso

Challenge fuels your learning process. A large part of the satisfaction of creative work comes from discovering something you didn't know before, pushing yourself beyond your limits, and developing new skills in the process.

Unfortunately, bad experiences at school lead many of us to associate learning with the pressure to pass tests and achieve grades—as we have seen, this kind of extrinsic motivation will kill your enjoyment, curiosity, and creativity. But the best teachers know this kind of education has nothing to do with learning. As Plutarch wrote in his *Moralia*, true learning is not the filling of a vessel but the kindling of a flame.

Learning has been embedded in creative production for centuries. In medieval Europe, craftsmen were required to go through a formal education process, administered by a guild or civic authority, starting as an **apprentice**. During their apprenticeship, they received food, lodging, and training from their master in return for labor. If they successfully completed their apprenticeship, they were awarded the status of **journeyman** and permitted to work for hire. Guild membership and the title of **master** were only awarded on production of a **masterpiece**—a piece of work of sufficient quality to merit the approval of judges within the guild.

Formal apprenticeships still survive in some creative professions. Others, such as architecture, where a high degree of technical competence is essential, require many years of training before students are certified to practice. Yet much of the learning in the modern creative professions takes place outside such formal structures: internships and mentorships with no official syllabus or examinations; influences absorbed from heroes and past masters; and discoveries from self-directed reading and learning via books, workshops, libraries, and the internet.

Some of the most inspiring creators are the ones who move from medium to medium, challenge to challenge, soaking up knowledge, and picking up skills as they go. Like Leonardo, who explored painting, sculpture, anatomy, engineering, architecture, music, cartography, and mathematics; or Mervyn Peake, who worked as an illustrator, painter, poet, novelist, sculptor, and playwright; or Picasso, who went through a succession of different "periods" as his style, media, and preoccupations shifted throughout his career; or David Bowie in the seventies, playing different characters and drawing on different genres, musical and visual styles, including folk, glam rock, soul, funk, music hall, electronica, mime, kabuki, the occult, science fiction, and performance art.

In the course of my own career I've learned a succession of different skills: poetry, literary criticism, editing, hypnosis, psychotherapy, coaching, presentation skills, productivity, copywriting, sales, blogging, html, online marketing, book publishing. Any one of those could have been a career in itself: I know people who are successful at each of them. Many of them are ongoing interests, but none of them is enough to satisfy me on its own. What *will* hold my attention for the rest of my life is the process of learning itself.

The more original and unusual your chosen path, the less likelihood that there will be a ready-made program of study waiting for you. As a creative professional, it is your responsibility to seek out the knowledge, skills, teachers, and mentors who can help you transform yourself from an enthusiastic beginner to a consummate master. This can be daunting, and you may find yourself going up a few blind alleys, but it's also exciting, and the information explosion of recent years means there has never been a bigger or better store of knowledge available to creators hungry for success.

Purpose

In Seth Godin's book *Tribes* he tells the story of being on holiday in Jamaica, unable to sleep and getting up at 4 a.m. to check his email in the hotel lobby. As he quietly minds his own business, a couple of partygoers roll in from a nightclub. One of them gives him a withering look and hisses:

> "Isn't it sad? That guy comes here on vacation and he's stuck checking his e-mail. He can't even enjoy his two weeks off."
> (*Tribes*, p.100)

The funny thing is, says Godin, "Other than sleeping, there was nothing I'd rather have been doing at that moment—because I'm lucky enough to have a job where I get to make change happen."

A sense of purpose—that your work matters, that it makes a difference in the world—is one of the most powerful motivators you can have. Even when you're not completely clear what your purpose is, or how you are going to fulfill it, it can give you the determination, even stubbornness, to keep going when things look hopeless to everyone else.

Around the same time I was agonizing over my poetry in that flat, I went out for a drink with a friend. The main topic of my conversation was my suffering: my struggles with business, with writing, with women. After listening patiently for longer than most people would, my friend made a kindly suggestion:

"If you're finding it so hard to succeed in your business, why don't you go back to publishing and get a job as an editor?"

To him, it was a reasonable solution to my problem, and a practical way to end my suffering. To me, it sounded totally insane. My work was *important*. I was on a *mission*. Why would I throw that away for a salary? *I was going to succeed at this*. Wasn't that obvious?

My friend smiled tactfully and went to the bar.

It's easy to see the life purpose in campaigners for change on a big scale: people like William Wilberforce, Mahatma Gandhi, Emmeline Pankhurst, Martin Luther King, Nelson Mandela, and Harvey Milk. They were so clear about their mission that they didn't have to get up in the morning and worry about "motivating" themselves. And if you feel called to make waves at that level, then go for it—it's a noble calling. But if not, don't overlook the difference you can make through your work—whether inspiring people with your art, helping them with your products or service, or lighting them up with your message.

It may be that your sense of purpose is right under your nose, if only you could see it: in my case, it turned out that part of my purpose in life is helping other creatives succeed without having to suffer as much as I used to.

Because it involves external results, you might be tempted to consider purpose an extrinsic motivation. But I'm not talking about a personal reward you receive for having done the work, but an effect that is integral to the work itself, that can affect people or situations beyond your usual sphere of influence. Nelson Mandela received the Nobel Peace Prize for his work to change South Africa. But that wasn't his motivation for doing it: the cause itself was his focus.

So is acting with purpose completely selfless action? Absolutely not. The sense of purpose *is* the reward.

Inspiration

Once upon a time it was taken for granted that the source of creativity was not the artist but the spirits, gods, or Muses, via inspiration. The word "inspiration" comes from the same Latin root as "respiration," suggesting that the artist "breathed in" influences from outside. The opening of Homer's *Odyssey* is a typical invocation to the Muse,[1] imploring the goddess to touch the poet with divine inspiration:

---

1 Most ancient Greek and Roman authors believed there were nine Muses, responsible for inspiring different art forms. Homer's Muse is believed to have been Calliope, the Muse of epic poetry.

Tell me, O Muse, th' adventures of the man
That having sack'd the sacred town of Troy,
Wander'd so long at sea; what course he ran
By winds and tempests driven from his way:
That saw the cities, and the fashions knew
Of many men, but suffer'd grievous pain
To save his own life, and bring home his crew;
Though for his crew, all he could do was vain,
They lost themselves by their own insolence,
Feeding, like fools, on the Sun's sacred kine;
Which did the splendid deity incense
To their dire fate. Begin, O Muse divine.

| Homer, *The Odyssey*, Book I, lines 1–12, translated by
   Thomas Hobbes

The tradition of invoking the Muse lasted a long time. Here is Milton going through the same ritual two-and-a-half thousand years later:

Of Man's first disobedience, and the fruit
Of that forbidden tree whose mortal taste
Brought death into the World, and all our woe,
With loss of Eden, till one greater Man
Restore us, and regain the blissful seat,
Sing, Heavenly Muse, that, on the secret top
Of Oreb, or of Sinai, didst inspire
That shepherd who first taught the chosen seed
In the beginning how the heavens and earth
Rose out of Chaos

| John Milton, *Paradise Lost*, Book I, lines 1–11

Milton was one of the last poets to invoke the Muse with a straight face. Even though his tone is sincere, there's a scholarly, antiquarian feel to his writing. While Homer's goddess sounds like a living, breathing reality, Milton's Muse sounds like someone he has only read about in a book.

A hundred years after Milton, with the Enlightenment in full swing, poets still paid lip service to the convention of invoking the Muse, but it had become a mere figure of speech, often delivered with smirking irony. By the 20th century, W.B. Yeats and Robert Graves were admired for their poetry but ridiculed for entertaining the idea of Muse-inspired sacred verse. Divine inspiration had been consigned to history, one of the "childish things" humankind put away when we grew up and became rational and scientific beings.

Then in 1976 psychologist Julian Jaynes published a startling book: *The Origin of Consciousness in the Breakdown of the Bicameral Mind.* He argued that ancient myths and legends of gods and spirits were not fiction in the modern sense, but descriptions of actual human experience. Because human consciousness was at an earlier stage of development, it was common for people to experience visual and auditory hallucinations. Instead of a unified conscious self, they had "bicameral" minds, divided into two parts: the first part gave instructions, in the form of hallucinated voices and images; the second part received the instructions and obeyed them, taking them for the speech of gods.

In support of his hypothesis Jaynes cited a mountain of evidence from ancient literature. For example, in the first book of the *Iliad,* when the goddess Athena appears to Achilles and tells him not to draw his sword and kill King Agamemnon, Homer was not indulging in a flight of fancy: one part of Achilles' bicameral mind was talking to the other, which he experienced as a hallucinated voice. The same goes for the many other ancient accounts of gods appearing to humans or speaking to them from shining clouds, burning bushes, pillars of fire, and so on. The storytellers weren't making it up. They, or the people they spoke of, really saw and heard these things. The theory sounds far fetched but it has been given serious consideration by such a hardcore rationalist as Richard Dawkins, in his book *The God Delusion*.

Jaynes argued that this ancient mode of thinking has to a large extent died out in modern society, but it survives here and there: in the people diagnosed as schizophrenics; in those who practice as mediums and claim to hear the voices of spirits; and in the many artists, writers, and other creators who have described inspiration coming to them in the form of hallucinated visions or voices.

The modern, vestigial form of inspiration tends not to be as dramatic and overpowering as the ancient one. Unless you are William Blake, you're unlikely to hear the voice of God or see angels walking down your street. It strikes in the form of an image or a phrase that pops into the mind as if from nowhere, and which is somehow loaded with significance for the artist. It's as though you have been given a clue to a mystery, or stumbled across a trail of breadcrumbs, inviting you to follow.

Like the time I was walking along a street in London and these words suddenly appeared in my mind:

We are living in the future

It's hardly high-flown poetry. Just a bald statement. But it buzzed with meaning for me. I remembered my boyhood in the seventies, when "the future" described by science fiction stories and movies seemed just around the corner. The main sci-fi comic was titled *2000 A.D.*, which according to my calculations, would fall within my lifetime—so I looked forward to experiencing the world of jet packs, lasers, and everyday interplanetary travel.

As those words appeared in my mind, I realized I was living in the future I had looked forward to as a child. But it wasn't quite what the comics and movies had predicted. Yes, I was surrounded by technological marvels, but the jet packs and space rockets seemed as far away as ever.

I turned the phrase over in my mind, inspecting it like an archaeologist who unearths a single roof tile and has to extrapolate from it an entire Roman villa or medieval guildhall. I only had a single line, but that gave me a lot. The voice was confident and optimistic, if slightly manic. I wasn't sure I trusted it. I wondered who "we" might be. The line was a regular trochaic tetrameter, giving me the form of all the other lines in the poem, as well as a pounding, insistent rhythm. It was a voice in a hurry. It almost certainly rhymed, probably in a very obvious, clanging way: probably couplets or quatrains. I played around with it, trying to catch the thought and follow it through, producing this:

> We are living in the future,
> you are living in the past.
> Your desires no longer matter:
> fall behind or catch up fast.

Looking at the line I had been given, and the ones I had written myself,[2] I couldn't see the join, which told me I had found the right form. Now I knew quite a few things about the voice: it was relentless, almost monotonous, like an advertising jingle repeated ad nauseam. It would feel no shame in recycling the same two rhymes for the entire poem (a digital rhyme scheme!). It wanted

2 The French poet Paul Valéry drew a distinction between *"les vers donnés"* (the given lines) and *"les vers calculés"* (the calculated lines). The first kind of line is "given" to the poet by inspiration, by his or her own genius, or simply by luck, and there is no question that it has found its true form. It then becomes a kind of touchstone or tuning fork for the second kind of line, which the poet "works out" as best he or she can.

to sweep the listener along with its breathless enthusiasm (or was it anxiety?) for the wonders of the modern age.

Because the voice proclaimed, "We are living in the future," I knew that everything in the poem had to have already happened, even if only recently. As the science fiction author William Gibson quipped, "The future is already here, it's just not very evenly distributed." So I combed my memory, news feeds, and the latest issue of *Wired* magazine for futuristic wonders that had already come to pass. This is what I came up with:[3]

The Future

We are living in the future,
you are living in the past.
Your desires no longer matter:
fall behind or catch up fast.

Asteroids are mined for water,
robots handle household tasks,
strangers swap electric scooters,
lovers wear full-body masks.

Gadgets learn to soothe and flatter:
passive phones, aggressive cars.
TVs gossip, fridges chatter,
bedside lights turn supergrass.

---

3 First published in *Magma Poetry*, issue 55.

Smart drugs upgrade old grey matter,
smart phones hold their owners' past,
sharp consumers sell their data,
switched-on poets leave no drafts.

Clubbers wear electric glitter,
monitor their lungs and heart,
satellites patrol the gutter,
homeless authors top the charts.

Tech and pharma take us further,
turn us into works of art:
seniors glow with youthful vigour,
test-tube mice glow in the dark.

Unmanned drones can fly forever,
laser snipers find their mark,
SeaBots home in underwater,
every target simulcast.

We are living in the future,
you are living in the past.
Our desires are all that matter:
catch up quick or fade out fast.

Creative flow

Have you ever had the experience of becoming so absorbed in your work that you tuned out your surroundings and lost track of time, when you felt a sense of effortlessness and pleasure in your work, even though you were producing more than usual?

This kind of experience is almost universal among creative people. Sadly, we don't experience it every day, but when we do it is unforgettable. It becomes one of our main motivations for doing what we do.

Psychologist Mihaly Csikszentmihalyi calls this state **creative flow**, which he describes as "an almost automatic, effortless, yet highly focused state of consciousness." Characteristics of creative flow include: having clear goals for your work; knowing how well you are doing; working on a challenge matched to your level of skill; an altered sense of time; intense focus, with distractions excluded from awareness; no worry of failure; absorption and pleasure in the work; and a lack of self-consciousness.

The good news is that in Csikszentmihalyi's research findings, described in his excellent book *Creativity: Flow and the Psychology of Discovery and Invention*, creative flow is strongly linked to high-level creative performance. Because it involves clear goals, feedback, and action, it is very different to daydreaming or letting your mind wander. And because flow feels good, it means pleasure is part of the job if you want to achieve great things as a creator.

You are likely to experience creative flow when the other types of intrinsic motivation combine to raise your level of performance. When you're aligned with your sense of purpose, doing work you love, setting yourself meaningful challenges, and developing your skills as you go, then creative flow is the natural result.

Obsession

In the documentary *Stanley Kubrick's Boxes*, presenter Jon Ronson, evidently a huge Kubrick fan, was invited to the director's home by his widow. What did he find when he got there? Cardboard boxes. Hundreds of them. Big ones, small ones, scruffy ones, neat ones. Boxes in the living room, boxes in the dining room, boxes in the study. Boxes in the outhouses, stacked from floor to ceiling.

Each box was labeled with the name or initials of one of Kubrick's movies, such as "EWS" (*Eyes Wide Shut*) or "FMJ" (*Full Metal Jacket*). And inside? Mostly photographs—endless variations on different objects and places. Bedside tables. Gates of country houses. Doorways to prostitutes' flats. Cafés. It was clearly source material for his movies, but on a mindbogglingly obsessive scale.

How many pictures of fancy dress shops do you need? Don't they all look pretty much the same? Evidently not to Kubrick. The director's nephew was introduced as principal photographer, recounting how he traipsed round every single fancy dress shop in south-east England to capture the required images.

On another occasion Kubrick decided he wanted photographs of every single building on Commercial Road in London so that he could lay them all side-by-side and inspect the entire road in his living room. But crucially, he didn't want perspective to get in the way—if taken from street level, the buildings would look tilted backwards and he wouldn't be able to line them up properly. So the photographer had to take a large ladder to Commercial Road, climb up twelve feet in the air, photograph the first building, then climb down, move the ladder along to the next building, and climb up to take the next photo. All along the road (it's not short). Both sides.

By conventional standards this qualifies as unusual behavior, but you can probably relate. You may not have quite so many boxes in your home, but you likely have a pretty decent collection relating to your creative passion—books, CDs, vinyl, DVDs, prints, sheet music, musical instruments, or drawing and painting paraphernalia. And you've doubtless indulged in what many people would class as obsession—working and reworking the same piece over and over, until you get it right. So you understand why Kubrick needed so many boxes. Why Jimi Hendrix needed forty takes to record "Gypsy Eyes." Why Robert De Niro needed to work as a taxi driver for several weeks in preparation for his role in *Taxi Driver*.

When I'm working on a poem, I will recite it in my head countless times until I've got it into a presentable state. (It's never finished, of course.) One of my current projects is a translation of Geoffrey Chaucer's masterpiece *Troilus and Criseyde* into modern English verse, preserving the original rhyme royal stanza form. I have five different editions of the poem, which is over 8,000 lines long. Each seven-line stanza takes several hours of work—on a good day. Sometimes I can spend hours on a single line, comparing the scholarly annotations in all five editions, and trying out different potential translations. How else am I supposed to get it right?

Obsession is probably essential for outstanding creative work—the ones who solve the biggest problems and create the most amazing things are the ones who won't let it go, who keep chipping away until they succeed. Up to a point, this is creative and fulfilling. But beyond a certain point, you start to suffer—it becomes harder to let the challenge go, to think of anything else, to switch off, to socialize, or to sleep at night. At this point, your work starts to suffer as much as you do, because you don't have the energy or mental clarity to do your best work.

Creators who have taken this to extremes have destroyed their relationships, careers, health, sanity, and even themselves. For the sake of your creativity as well as your self, it's important to recognize the early warning signals that you are becoming more obsessive than creative:

- A feeling that you can't stop working, or thinking about work
- Constant dissatisfaction with everything you create—beyond even your usual high standards
- Difficulty relaxing
- Friends and colleagues tell you (repeatedly) that you need to take a break
- Insomia
- Compulsive behavior—over-indulging in food, drink, sex, TV, shopping, gambling, etc.
- Feeling physically run down or burnt out

These are all prompts to take time out and get some perspective on things. Sometimes a weekend break or a holiday can make all the difference. If the symptoms are more serious, consider consulting your doctor or a therapist.

When you're caught up in obsessive behavior, it feels impossible to let go of your work—but I've seen plenty of creatives reach a turning point when they realize that their creativity will benefit from taking a break and building regular downtime into their working habits.

CHAPTER 7

Finding inspiration

Now we've considered the different types of intrinsic motivation, here are some practical steps you can take to encourage inspiration to strike.

65

- **Do something that inspires you**
- **Follow your curiosity**
- **Eliminate distractions (especially rewards)**
- **Sharpen your critical faculty**
- **Keep challenging yourself**
- **Reclaim your soul**

Do something that inspires you

This is the big one. Unless you are doing this, all the motivation techniques in the world won't make any difference.

When I start writing a poem, I'm stepping into the same space as my poetic heroes, including Chaucer, Shakespeare, Coleridge, Eliot, Bishop, Plath, Auden, MacNeice, Hughes, and Larkin. Trying to do the same thing they did. Intimidating? Of course. Exciting? The word doesn't even come close.

The same goes for you, when you commit to a creative discipline that has inspired you from the beginning—whether in the arts, science, invention, teaching, entrepreneurship, or another field. You are following in the footsteps of your heroes.

Here are some questions to help you find the sweet spot between inspiring and scary in your work.

- What inspires you about the work you do?
- What is the most inspiring thing you could do with your life? Are you doing it (yet)?
- Who are your creative heroes? How high did they aim? Are you aiming that high?

If you feel yourself hesitating—why? What's stopping you? Here are some of the most common reasons I hear from clients:

- **False modesty:** "Who am I to think I could do this?"
- **Tomorrowism:** "I'm going to get started on it one day…"
- **Fear disguised as common sense:** "I need to earn a living… I don't have time…"
- **Missing inner qualities:** "I don't have the talent/motivation/confidence/whatever."
- **Missing external resources:** "I don't have the education/money/connections/whatever."
- **The Inner Critic:** "I'm not good enough."

These are all powerful excuses, and they are all lies. They are just stories you tell yourself in your head. They have nothing to do with reality. The day you stop telling yourself this kind of story and commit yourself to doing what *really* inspires you, is the day your journey begins in earnest.

Follow your curiosity

If you are struggling to identify the big thing that inspires you, then start small—with curiosity.

I once attended a writing class with the poet Craig Raine where he compared writing poetry to stripping wallpaper. When you scrape a piece of wallpaper, you end up with a little "tag" of wallpaper sticking out. When you pull, sometimes the tag breaks off in your hand and you need to scrape again. Other times, you pull the tag and it gets bigger and bigger, till a long strip of wallpaper comes away in your hands. Sometimes the strip goes on and on until you've pulled away the paper from a whole section of wall—like surprising yourself by writing an epic. If you hadn't been curious enough to pull the little tag, you'd never have managed such a spectacular achievement (in either wallpaper-stripping or poetry).

Follow your curiosity wherever you find it—lots of times it will trickle out, but if you keep trying, sooner or later you'll feel it swell to a rushing torrent of inspiration.

To help you get started, look out for the "tags" in your life that are piquing your curiosity:

- A book you've been meaning to read?
- A movie on your watchlist?
- Something you've always wanted to learn?
- An idea you never got around to trying out?
- A person you've been meaning to call?

Eliminate distractions (especially rewards)

The power of intrinsic motivation is the power of focus: when you do something out of love, you give it all your attention, doing whatever it takes to make it the best you can do. Or the other way round: the more you eliminate distractions and focus, the more likely you are to experience intrinsic motivation.

There are several ways to eliminate distractions. In today's hyperconnected world, it generally pays to use them in combination!

- **Scheduling:** block out time on your calendar for your creative work. Resist the temptation to schedule meetings or other appointments during this time.
- **Rules:** write the rules of your own game—decide what you are allowed and not allowed to do during your creative time. Obvious things to avoid include answering email or the phone, or using Facebook. I recommend avoiding secondary activities such as research or preparing your materials or studio. Focus on actually *creating* something during this time.
- **Artful vagueness:** *don't* tell people "I can't meet on Wednesday, I'm writing/painting/composing." Unless they are a creator themselves, they won't understand. Just tell them you're not available.
- **Forget the rewards!** It's fine to daydream about playing to sell-out crowds, hitting the bestseller lists, or winning an Oscar—just don't do it during your creative work time.
- **Technology:** if you need to work on the computer and willpower is not enough to keep you away from distracting websites, use software such as AntiSocial (Anti-Social.cc), MacFreedom (MacFreedom.com), or Focus (HeyFocus.com) to lock you out of certain sites (or the entire internet) for the duration of your work session.

- **Ritual:** many creatives have a warm-up ritual to help them start work. It can be as simple as making your favorite coffee and putting on some background music, or an elaborate sequence of yoga, meditation, and visualization (goat sacrifices optional). It might seem illogical, but this kind of ritual works by association—your unconscious mind learns to associate the ritual with the creative state of mind in which you do your best work.

Sharpen your critical faculty

One of the conditions of flow identified by Csikszentmihalyi is having high-quality feedback about how well you are performing in relation to your goal. Which presents a problem when it comes to creative work. If you are an athlete, racing against your competitors with a crowd roaring you on gives you loud, clear, and immediate feedback. This helps top athletes enter what they call "the zone." But if you are creating an art installation, or writing an experimental symphony, or a lyric poem, you may have to wait months or even years for feedback—and even then it may be unclear or contradictory, as experts routinely disagree about the merits of a work of art. No wonder so many artists give up in frustration.

The solution, according to Csikszentmihalyi, is to learn as much as possible about your creative field and develop your own critical faculty to the point where you can *give yourself feedback* as you work. In accounts of their working habits, many great creators describe devoting time to assessing and revising their work:

> "What has been set down in a moment of ardor must now be critically examined, improved, extended, or condensed, as the form

requires. Sometimes one must do oneself violence, must sternly and pitilessly take part against oneself, before one can mercilessly erase things thought out with love and enthusiasm."

| Peter Ilich Tchaikovsky, Letter, 25 June (7 July) 1878, edited by Rosa Newmarch

In my book *Resilience* I outlined eight ways you can sharpen your critical faculty.

1. **Get to know the major creators and works in your field**— even the unfashionable ones, and the ones you think you won't like
2. **Read reviews with a critical eye**—so that you identify the reviewers' criteria, assumptions, and biases.
3. **Read critics and practitioners**—critical books, studies, reviews, journals, as well as creators reflecting on their art.
4. **Debate with friends**—this forces you to think hard about your opinions and how to justify them!
5. **Join a workshop or discussion group**—MeetUp.com is a good place to start looking for one.
6. **Contribute to a forum**—whatever your interest there is almost certainly a forum, Facebook group, or similar online gathering devoted to it.
7. **Start a blog or podcast**—a great way to articulate your ideas and test them in debate with others.
8. **Benchmark against the best**—stretch yourself by comparing your work to the very best that has been produced in your field.

Keep challenging yourself

As a self-starting creative, you're responsible for setting your own challenges. So make sure they are big enough to inspire you (and scare you).

Remember, one of Csikszentmihalyi's conditions of flow is a dynamic balance between the **difficulty** of a challenge and your **ability**: if the challenge is too easy, you get bored; if too hard, you get frustrated. Flow occurs at the sweet spot where you are stretching yourself to achieve the previously-impossible.

If you're feeling bored and dissatisfied with your life, set yourself a big challenge—the kind that gets your pulse racing and keeps you up at night. Maybe you are pretty good at what you do and you have experienced a certain level of success—but whatever level you are at, you can find someone doing it at a higher level. What's to stop *you* aiming that high?

On the other hand, if you are struggling and getting frustrated, maybe you are putting unrealistic pressure on yourself to succeed too quickly. Sometimes you need to slow down and master the basics—really master them—before you are ready to work at the advanced level.

The great thing about challenges is you can always make them bigger. Which means you have a lifetime's source of fulfillment at your fingertips.

Reclaim your soul

"I got everything I wanted and I'm still not happy."

Max certainly didn't look happy. Behind him on my iPad I could see a line of mountains in the sunshine. It was a beautiful day. But his face was like thunder.

When I started coaching Max, he had shown me photos of the stunning landscape where he lived and painted. He had told me of his dream, growing up as a city kid, of moving to the wilderness as a well-known artist with collectors vying for his work. He had made it all happen. But he had come to me for help because the pressure of money and success had caused him to stop painting.

"Whatever I churn out, someone will pay five figures because it has my name on it. It makes the whole thing meaningless."

Max readily admitted it was a first world problem, and criticized himself severely for having so much and enjoying it so little. But that didn't help.

When I asked him to tell me how he became a painter, he became gradually more animated, describing his life as an art student who painted "for the hell of it." Working all night when the rest of the city was asleep, then watching them crowd onto rush hour buses before he retired to bed for the day.

"I was nobody then, but I was happier than I am now."

We decided it was time for him to become nobody again. I asked him to imagine drawing a magic circle around his studio to protect it from outside influences. (He actually marked the circle out with stones, in a ceremonial "reconsecrating" of the space.) Once he stepped inside the circle, he was nobody once more, and nothing he did was of any consequence. He could create for the hell of it, and destroy it afterwards if he wanted.

The golden rule was to create *with no plan to show the work to another human being*—let alone sell it. No one would ever know what he created inside the circle—unless, after storing it unseen for at least three months, he decided he wanted to use it professionally.

One of the other things we did was to reorganize his day so that making art was hermetically sealed from the business of art. Mornings, evenings, (and maybe the middle of the night) were for painting. Email, phone calls, and meetings were confined to a window in the afternoons between 2 p.m. and 5 p.m.

Over the next few weeks the old Max returned. He smiled mischievously as he described some of the "insane stuff" he produced in studio sessions, including two all-nighters. Sometimes he showed me a piece, grinning as he told me the galleries would have to wait.

By the time the works came out of three months in "cold storage," he saw them differently. From this perspective, he could judge them better. Some he liked and wanted to keep. Some he liked and wanted to sell. Some he painted over.

A nice side effect of putting fewer works on the market meant that shortage of supply pushed his prices up. An exhibition the following year sold out in record time. Max was pleased about this, but said it was nothing compared to "having my art back."

If you've achieved a certain amount of professional success and your creativity is threatened by the weight of expectation—from your fans, advisers, and/or yourself—here are some suggestions for reclaiming your artistic soul.

1. Ask yourself: *"Why do I do this?"* and write down all the answers that come to mind.

If you come up with any extrinsic rewards, like the ones below, then cross them out and dig deeper until you get to a reason you feel in your bones.

- Money
- Fame
- Reputation
- Awards
- Praise
- Opportunity

2. Now think back to a specific time in the past when you really enjoyed creating, and produced work you were happy with.

- When did you fall in love with your art?
- What was exciting about it?
- How did it feel when you were "nobody" and could create whatever you liked, with no one watching?

3. Spend time with your early works to help yourself reconnect with the feelings that went into them. Revisit your original sources of inspiration—places you went, books you read, movies you watched. Play that album you haven't listened to in years.

4. Put "hard edges" in your day to separate creative and business activities—e.g. creating in the morning, meetings in the afternoon. Respect the boundaries!

5. Find a dedicated space for your creative work that is separate from your business office. It could be your own studio or a public space like a library or shared studio.

Imagine drawing a magic circle around your workspace. If it's your own space, feel free to *actually* mark a circle around it in a creative ritual. (Best not to do this at the public library!)

6. When you step inside the circle, you are nobody—and nothing you make is of any consequence. You are free to create whatever you like, without worrying about quality, marketability, or what anyone else will think. *No one will ever know* what you create— unless you later decide you want to share it.

Work from the inside out, going with whatever arouses your curiosity, regardless of external considerations.

7. Whatever you produce, store it for at least three months. During that time, do not show it to anyone else. You are free to look at it yourself, but not to make any firm decisions about what to do with it. Having this time limit will insert a "buffer" between creating and promoting, so that they do not interfere with each other.

When the three months are up, take the work out and consider it.

- Do you like it?
- Do you want to keep it?
- Do you want to share or sell it?
- Do you want to trash it and start something else?

INTRINSIC MOTIVATION

Resistance:
the shadow side of joy

After focusing on the Joy of Work and the wonderful creative benefits of intrinsic motivation, you might be experiencing a nagging thought at the back of your mind:

"It's great to know that creativity can be enjoyable, and I do get that feeling sometimes, but not always. And if I'm supposed to love my creative work, how come I spend so much time procrastinating and avoiding it?"

Good question. I've been there myself, many times. And as a coach for creative people who tell me what's *really* going on in their working lives, I assure you procrastination is an epidemic in the creative industries. It's one of the paradoxes of creativity that we choose to follow our passion and do the work we love—yet when it comes to the point of getting down to work, we suddenly find ourselves compelled to check email or Facebook, phone a friend, catch up with our accounts, or clean out the cupboard under the sink—anything but the very thing we claim to love so much!

So what's going on here?

This is the question bestselling novelist Steven Pressfield addresses in his books for creators, *The War of Art* and *Turning Pro*. What holds us back, he says, is an invisible, insidious, internal force he calls **Resistance**. When I asked him to elaborate on this idea, he was kind enough to answer a few questions.

AN INTERVIEW WITH STEVEN PRESSFIELD, AUTHOR

What is Resistance?

If you've ever paid hundreds of quid for a treadmill and brought it home only to have it gather dust in the attic, you know what Resistance is. Resistance is that negative force that radiates off the blank page for writers, the blank canvas for painters, and the blank screen for filmmakers. Resistance is self-sabotage. It's fear. It's timorousness and irresolution. Resistance is the voice in your head that tells you you're not good enough, not smart enough, not sexy enough—and besides, everything that's any good has already been done and who would want to hear what pitiful insights you could bring to the party?

Resistance is invisible, intractable, impersonal, insidious, indefatigable. Resistance never quits. Nor does defeating it get any easier with experience and time. The dragon must be slain anew every morning (and at every interval throughout the day).

Another way to look at Resistance is that it is the shadow that is cast by the tree of our creative dream. Resistance arises second. The dream comes first. As soon as our soul hatches a creative idea or vision, either for a worthy project that we might undertake or for an evolution in our personal and moral life, Resistance appears. The tree is the dream. Resistance is its shadow. That's why I say Resistance is impersonal. It's a law of nature, like gravity or the transit of Venus. Resistance's apparition is almost Newtonian, in the sense of an "equal and opposite reaction" to the vision or impulse to ascend to a higher level creatively, morally, or spiritually.

Rule of thumb: the more important an activity or enterprise is to the positive evolution of our souls, the more Resistance we will feel toward beginning (and completing) that enterprise. In a way this is good. We can use it like a compass to determine what course of action we should take. Faced with multiple alternative projects ("Should I do A, B, or C?") we can simply ask ourselves, "Which one am I most afraid of? To which project do I feel the most Resistance?"

That's the one we should (and must) do.

Isn't it odd that Resistance appears when we decide to pursue the thing we want to achieve the most? Why is that?

Some very smart people have identified Resistance with the "lizard brain," the amygdala, and have suggested that it serves the evolutionary purpose of preventing the human race from trying out dangerous, new ideas. The lizard brain likes the status quo; it will always say, "Don't do that!" There may be some truth to this hypothesis, but it doesn't resonate with me.

At the risk of sounding too apocalyptic, I would associate Resistance much more closely with "evil." In Jewish mysticism (Kabbala), the force that I call Resistance is called the *"yetzer hara,"* which means "a turning toward evil." It's in Genesis. It's one of the reasons God decided to send the Great Flood. Have I lost you yet?

In all seriousness, I think Resistance is simply the shadow to creativity's sun. One part of our nature as humans summons us to flight. Gravity resists. It's a law of nature. One part of our nature calls us to create, to bring into being "that which is not yet," in other words to take on the role normally reserved only for gods. Some force resists that. Heaven itself?

What's the single most important thing we need to do to overcome Resistance?

Because Resistance is entirely self-spawned and self-perpetuated (we fuel it by our own fear of it), Resistance can be overcome by force of will. Mental toughness. How does the knight slay the dragon? By overcoming his own fear and advancing to battle.

The metaphor that worked for me in my own life as a writer was the idea of "turning pro." I like this way of looking at the issue because it eliminates all self-judgment. We are not "wrong" if we feel Resistance. We are not "ill." We are simply looking at the problem as amateurs. As soon as we "turn pro," even if only within our own minds, the battle becomes quite winnable.

Consider the differences in attitude between an amateur and a pro. An amateur dabbles. He is not in it for the long haul. He collapses at the first hint of adversity. An amateur is arrogant, precious; his ego is wedded to his progress. He is brittle. He has no staying power. He is not committed, heart and soul. The professional on the other hand rises each morning ready to face the blank canvas. She is committed. She can endure adversity and even thrive on it. The professional's ego is not attached to her "instrument." She can withstand delay and criticism and defeat. She is in it for the long haul. She is mentally tough.

Step One in overcoming Resistance is to acknowledge its existence. Yes, there is a negative force, and yes, that force is formidable and relentless. To defeat it we must marshal our sternest resources of self-discipline, self-motivation, self-reinforcement, and self-validation. We must be like Ernest Shackleton or Edmund Hillary. Neither of them became "Sirs" because they were spiritual cream puffs.

Another way to look at this is that to overcome Resistance, we need to develop our own "interior culture." Big organizations have institutional cultures. Apple has a culture; the SAS has a culture; Manchester United has a culture. These cultures consist of self-conceptions ("Someone like us acts only in such-and-such a way"), levels of aspiration ("Someone like us aims only for the top"), and standards of achievement ("Someone like us will not accept work at any level short of the very best").

You and I as artists and entrepreneurs must develop our own personal interior cultures. We must cultivate and reinforce the virtues of these cultures (the virtues of a professional) and relentlessly work to eradicate the vices (fear, self-doubt, etc.). These internal cultures are our lance and our armor. Saint George had an interior culture. That's what he used to slay the dragon.

StevenPressfield.com

Resisting Resistance

From following Steve's advice, working on my own Resistance, and helping clients overcome theirs, I've found the following three principles particularly effective:

LIMIT YOUR OPTIONS

This one builds on the idea of scheduling creative work time. At the start of each week, I will look at my diary, notice what times I have blocked out for writing, and mentally commit to writing at those times. This means that when it's time to get to work, I have only two options: to follow through on my commitment, or to give in to Resistance.

If I let myself decide each day whether or not to write, Resistance could kid me that I will get round to it "later" or "tomorrow." But having made the decision beforehand, I know that when the time comes, I will either be writing or avoiding writing. One less crack in the day for Resistance to squeeze through.

KNOW YOUR ENEMY

When I sat down to write this morning, it was hard to settle at first—I found myself itching to check my email, to look up a book on Amazon, then watch the video of James Rodriguez' amazing goal for Colombia against Uruguay in the World Cup. Then I realized what was happening:

"OK this is Resistance. It must be time to get to work."

Just seeing that clearly made all the difference. I knew what I was avoiding, so it was hard to kid myself any longer. I needed to close the browser, open up Scrivener, and start writing. It takes self-awareness to spot Resistance in the moment. One way to develop this is to make a game of "Resistance spotting": observe yourself during the day and look out for the behaviors—procrastination, surfing the web, tidying up—that indicate that Resistance is on the prowl.

LOOK AT THE BIG PICTURE

One of Resistance's sneakiest tricks is to persuade you that your time is not precious, and that it won't make much difference if you fool around for a few more minutes, or if you take the day off, or get started tomorrow instead of today. *"There's plenty of time,"* it whispers. *"Why stress yourself out?"*

The antidote to this is to look at the big picture and to see—really *see*—the link between what you do today and what you will achieve with your only life. If I don't start writing my book till tomorrow, it feels like it won't make a big difference. But the longer I look at it like that, the more I keep putting the book off …and weeks or months can pass with no book in sight.

The people I meet who are creating the most amazing things are the ones with a sense of urgency about their life. They don't panic, but they see each day for what it is: a precious, never-to-be-repeated opportunity to bring something extraordinary into the world. Which means they can't wait to get started.

Beyond Resistance: true fulfillment

Remember what Csikszentmihalyi says about challenge and flow? If there were no challenge, no difficulty, no Resistance, no inner demons to confront, or dragons to slay, there would be no real achievement, and no real fulfillment.

It's one thing to enjoy your work when things are going well, and I wish you plenty of days like that. But when you face up to internal Resistance and external obstacles and overcome them both, it brings a whole different order of fulfillment—you have to dig deep, you learn things about yourself that you could not learn in any other way, and when you finally succeed, it is far more satisfying than if you had had an easy ride. That's the kind of fulfillment I wish for you most of all.

EXTRINSIC MOTIVATION
Rewards for Work

EXTRINSIC MOTIVATION

CHAPTER 9

Rewards for work

"No man but a blockhead ever wrote, except for money."
| Samuel Johnson

"Believe me that my sole purpose is to make as much money as
possible, which, next to health, is best of all."
| Wolfgang Amadeus Mozart, *Letters*[1]

"You fools! I am a poor goldsmith, who serves whoever pays me."
| Benvenuto Cellini, *Autobiography*

Are you shocked by these frank admissions of financial ambition
from esteemed artists? Or at least a little disappointed?
 If so, why?
 Stop and think about this before you read on.

Does your perception change when I tell you that Johnson endured
several periods of poverty, including having to leave university

---

1 Mozart was writing to his father, so he may well have exaggerated his focus
 on money to present himself in a responsible light. But there's no doubt
 Mozart was fond of money and the pleasures it could buy.

without completing his degree, due to lack of funds? Or when I remind you that Mozart died penniless and was buried in a pauper's grave?[2]

If so, why does *that* make a difference to the way you see them?

Maybe it doesn't bother you whether artists are rich or poor, ambitious for money or not. But many of us have an unconscious association between riches and greed, and poverty and virtue. A starving artist seems somehow purer than a rich celebrity. So we idolize Vincent van Gogh and feel uncomfortable when modern artists are paid a fortune for stacks of bricks or unmade beds.

Show me a professional artist or creative with no ambition, and I'll show you a liar. No matter how much we may love our art for its own sake, very few of us will turn our noses up at the rewards on offer. These rewards are known as **extrinsic motivations**, because they are external to the work itself. In many creative fields the extrinsic rewards are so spectacular that competition is cut-throat and hordes of young hopefuls are prepared to invest huge amounts of time, effort, and energy for a shot at the big time.

"But hang on a minute—haven't you been saying that intrinsic motivation is critical for creative success? And that creative professionals are more motivated by the joy of work than by money?"

Absolutely. If you want to produce outstanding creative work, then *while you are working* you need to be 100 per cent focused on the task in hand. But that doesn't mean you don't care about the rewards. In fact, if you're a creative professional, you *have* to care about the rewards.

---

2 In spite of earning a lot of money, Mozart's fortunes fluctuated throughout his career. Some of this was down to his spendthrift habits, but he also faced challenging circumstances including expensive medical treatment for his wife's illness. For more on Mozart and money, visit: Mozart.com/en/timeline/life/mozart-and-money

If you're an employee or freelancer, you can't just sit around doodling whatever you like. You're under constant pressure from your boss or clients to produce dazzling creative work, to specifications, and on time. You can't afford to ignore money—you need to speak up for what you want and negotiate payment that reflects the value you create.

If you're an independent artist, you can create whatever you like. But you also need to find buyers for your work. Success brings still more pressure, as you strive to keep surprising and delighting your fans.

If you're a creative entrepreneur, the market can be merciless. You can't just please yourself—you *need* to anticipate and satisfy your customers' needs and desires, otherwise your company is toast.

Even in an art like my own—poetry—where there's little money or fame to be had, there are plenty of other rewards to distract you from your true calling: publication, awards, reviews, praise, and criticism. These constitute your artistic or critical reputation, which many people prize more than popularity.

RICH ARTIST, POOR ARTIST

Supposing we played a game and picked two teams, one composed of great artists who earned fortunes in their own lifetimes, and the other of artists who struggled financially in spite of producing what is now recognized as great work.

The first team could include William Shakespeare, George Frideric Handel, Pablo Picasso, Charles Dickens, and Giuseppe Verdi, all of whom made it their business to make good money from their creative work. For the poor team we could pick Vincent van Gogh, Franz Schubert, Amedeo Modigliani, John Keats, and Johannes Vermeer. The fact that their work has earned millions posthumously is no consolation to them, and shows that artistic merit does not guarantee financial security.

Judging the teams on artistic merit, it would be hard to separate the two: we might disagree about individuals, but across both teams there is such a wealth of undisputed creative achievement that there would be no clear winner. If the psychologists and Romantics are right, all of the artists on both teams had very high levels of intrinsic motivation, since it is impossible to achieve outstanding creative work without it.

When it comes to external markers of success, however, the first team is a clear winner. And not just in financial terms: their income was directly related to the fame and artistic reputation they achieved, since it depended on the number of tickets (Shakespeare), or books (Dickens), they sold, or the high prices their reputation commanded (Picasso, Verdi, Handel).

The rich team shows it is possible to "have it all" as a creator: to gain money, fame, and reputation during your lifetime by producing outstanding creative work. Somehow they managed to combine intrinsic and extrinsic motivations in such a way that they did not conflict but were mutually reinforcing.

THE PARADOX OF CREATIVE MOTIVATION

The relationship between creativity, intrinsic motivation, and extrinsic motivation presents creators with a paradox:

The more you focus on intrinsic motivation, the more creative and original your work will be. And the better your work, the easier it will be to earn rewards from it.

But the more you focus on extrinsic motivation, the less creative and original your work will be. And the poorer your work, the harder it will be to earn rewards from it.

So if your main motivation is to be rich and famous from creative work, it will be harder to become rich and famous than if your main motivation is to create great work, regardless of rewards.

I am *not* saying creating great work is all you need: unless you are one of the very few who hit the big time with no apparent

EXTRINSIC MOTIVATION

effort, you will also need to promote your work, or have someone do this for you.

And yes, it's possible to make a lot of money in some markets with mediocre work and stellar marketing. But if you have a discerning audience—and if you're reading this book, I assume that's what you want—stellar marketing works better with a stellar product.

HOW SUCCESSFUL CREATIVES RESOLVE THE PARADOX

Having coached hundreds of creatives at different stages of their career and different levels of success, I've heard a lot about what motivates them, including their innermost thoughts, doubts, and ambitions. Here's what I've learned from them about the mindset it takes to succeed professionally and financially, as well as creatively.

They all love their work. I've never worked with a creative professional whose eyes do not light up when we start talking about this.

Young or old, rich or poor, everyone wants money. Some are conflicted—e.g. they want money, but feel they don't "deserve it," or they think rich people are "bad" in some way, and don't want to be like that. But they most definitely want money.

And they nearly all want some combination of fame and reputation. Some are happy with what they have, while others wish they were more famous. ("People who know tell me my work is amazing, so how come no one has heard of me?") Or had a higher artistic reputation. ("Just because I'm well known, the critics turn up their noses at me.")

The people who are the *least* successful at reaping the rewards for their work are usually doing one of two things:

1. **Focusing *exclusively* on intrinsic motivation**—ignoring rewards and pretending that they don't matter, or that they will magically appear in response to great work. "Do what

you love and the rest will follow" is a popular mantra with this group.

2. **Obsessing about extrinsic motivation**—either daydreaming about success (and doing nothing to make it happen) or complaining about the lack of money, fame, opportunities, and recognition in their lives.

Some of them flip from one to the other as anxiety, hopefulness, and resentment take turns to run the show. In this scenario, the creative motivation paradox turns into a vicious circle.

The people who are *most* successful at combining creative achievement with financial and professional success have a very different focus of attention:

1. **Focusing *primarily* on intrinsic motivation**—especially during dedicated work time. They work on their craft every day, often first thing in the morning, giving it their best energy and attention.

2. **Focusing strategically on extrinsic motivation**—especially when it comes to making big picture decisions about their career. They devote significant time and energy to reward-generating activities such as networking, promotion, marketing, sales, and negotiation.

In this scenario, intrinsic and extrinsic motivations support each other: because the creatives devote most of their attention to intrinsic motivation, they are happier, their work is continually improving, and their promotional efforts have greater impact. And because they are earning extrinsic rewards, they are freer to focus on their craft without worrying about money or recognition.

Their creative projects also benefit from the funding, connections, and opportunities they have generated. The creative motivation paradox resolves into a virtuous circle.

94

EXTRINSIC MOTIVATION

CHAPTER 10

Types of extrinsic motivation

Money, fame, and artistic reputation are the three biggest rewards
available to creators. Their relative importance to you will depend
on your creative field and personal inclinations. They are valuable
not just in their own right, but also because they lead to bigger
and better opportunities in your career.

- **Money**
- **Fame**
- **Reputation**
- **Opportunity**

Money

> "When bankers get together they talk about art. When artists get
> together, they talk about money."
> | Oscar Wilde

Sometimes we say, "Money doesn't matter," but deep down we know
this is not true. It may not matter in the same way love, art, and
world peace matter, but that's beside the point. It may not matter
in the way we'd like it to—with artists and nurses being paid as
much as bankers and property developers—but that doesn't mean
it doesn't matter. Money may be abused in all sorts of ways—but
that still doesn't mean it doesn't matter.

If you've ever lain awake at night worrying about how you will pay next month's bills, then you know money matters.

If you've ever said "no" to a wonderful experience—such as a holiday, a day at the spa, or a meal with friends at a nice restaurant—because you couldn't afford it, then you know money matters.

If you've ever sold something you've created yourself—even for a few dollars—then you know money matters.

If you've ever been paid a lot of money for one of your creations and seen the buyer's face light up with pleasure at their purchase—then you know money matters.

So what's the right attitude for a creator towards money? Given that it's an extrinsic reward, surely that makes it a creativity killer, something to be avoided?

Yes and no.

If you see money as a static thing, an end goal, an incentive, something to "get," then yes, focusing on this will kill your creativity—especially if you do it when you're actually executing your work. So when you're creating in the studio, or at your desk, or in front of your audience or client, money should be banished from your mind.

On the other hand, one of the many wonderful things about being creative is that there is virtually no limit to the value we can create for others, and therefore potentially no limit on the money we can generate. Just look at the fees and royalties paid to the most successful painters, designers, actors, musicians, authors, architects, and other creatives.

Forget about "earning money," it sounds too much like drudgery. Instead, focus on *creating value*.

And when you create a lot of value—for your audience, your employer, or your customers—why *shouldn't* you enjoy the rewards? But you have probably noticed it's not a simple case of doing amazing work and letting people see the value for themselves: you need to *show* them the value, by communicating clearly and confidently—whether in sales meetings, salary negotiations, or your marketing communications.

When coaching creatives, over and over I have noticed that mindset is crucial to translating creative talent into professional and financial success. Those who "just want to create" and lack the confidence to ask for money, market their work, or set their prices according to their true value, are the ones who struggle. They work longer hours for less reward, feeling discouraged, anxious, and resentful—and their creativity suffers as much as they do.

The irony is that those who are honest with themselves about their financial ambitions and bold enough to promote their work and charge healthy fees, are the ones who spend most time thinking about their art: like Wilde's bankers, money is not a worry for them, they are happy with their remuneration and confident of the value they create—leaving them free to focus on doing what they love.

Fame

Fame is a huge motivation for millions of would-be superstars: when everyone knows your name, when you see it in the papers, in the Broadway lights, or trending on Twitter, it is easy to feel you are having an impact and making a difference. Even if you don't yearn to see your name in lights, you are probably not averse to a bit of public recognition for your efforts. An appreciative round of applause after a performance, a glowing review of your latest work, or an appreciative Tweet from a stranger can make your day and send you back to work with fresh enthusiasm.

Andy Warhol said, "In the future, everyone will be famous for fifteen minutes," and in a way he was right: now, anyone can set up a blog, podcast, or social media account and start attracting an audience. In the pre-internet era, there was a large gulf between the people "in the media" and the rest of us. But this brave new online world has made the gulf small enough to step over, and introduced several lower levels of fame—which I call **young hopeful**, **midlister**, and **social media star**—before you reach the heights of international celebrity, when the big media pick you up and make you a **household name**.

YOUNG HOPEFUL

At this stage you are just starting out, publishing the first few posts on your blog, videos on YouTube, podcasts on iTunes, or images on Instagram, and seeing people start to notice your work. You start receiving comments and emails from strangers. I remember checking my website stats shortly after I started blogging, and noticing with excitement that other bloggers were starting to link to my blog, and that I was seeing a small but unmistakable rise in the number of daily visitors: strangers were *paying attention to my writing*. It was magical, like writing a book and seeing people reading it.

Even if you are only famous to fifteen people, their feedback can encourage you to redouble your efforts. The effect is usually positive—the novelty value makes it fun, and with such small numbers, it's hard to have delusions of grandeur.

MIDLISTER

In book publishing, "midlist author" means someone who sells enough books to justify continuing publication without breaking out with a big hit. I'm using the term midlister to describe someone who has attracted a large enough audience to earn a living from their creative work and/or to make a significant impact on their field of expertise. By any normal standards, I'm not remotely famous. No one recognizes me when I walk down the street. Yet in the past year, over 400,000 people have visited my websites. Over 15,000 people currently subscribe to my mailing lists. I know hardly any of these people personally, but they know who I am. Each time I speak at a conference, I meet people who tell me they have been reading my writing for a while and have been looking forward to meeting me. It's a little disconcerting, but also fun.

At the midlist level, you receive many of the benefits of fame—audience, opportunities, sales, a sense that you are having an impact—without the drawbacks of true fame. Inevitably, you attract criticism as well as praise. You encounter the occasional troll. You receive a steady stream of requests from strangers asking you to do favors for them, such as promoting their product on your website. But the attention and demands of the outside world are not relentless. The flow of information is manageable.

On the other hand, you can easily make the situation worse for yourself. Social media addiction can become a problem. As activity across your digital networks grows, so does the temptation to keep checking your phone for updates—making it harder to focus on your creative work. Resistance rubs its hands with glee. If you are always online, you never truly relax.

SOCIAL MEDIA STAR

Above the midlisters stand the internet celebrities, with hundreds of thousands of followers on social media. These are the people who have made it their business to master the new currencies of fame, and succeeded spectacularly.

Many of the opportunities and challenges are similar to those of the midlist, but at higher volume and velocity. You experience the instant gratification of seeing ripples online whenever you post something new, and the excitement of a rush of sales when you launch a new product or event. The opportunities that land in your inbox are more flattering and lucrative. On the flipside, you are more likely to be a target for trolls and stalkers. The stream of requests swells to a flood of demands. It is impossible to keep up with all the digital communications, so you delegate some of these.

The temptation to stay connected becomes stronger: how can you concentrate on your work when who knows what social media storms may have blown up in the last few minutes? In some ways this is even more intense than traditional fame: even if you objectively have fewer fans than a Hollywood star of the seventies, they are closer to you. Instead of keeping your audience at bay behind the gates of your mansion, you carry them with you on your phone wherever you go. Burning a hole in your pocket. On the table as you eat. By the chair as you relax with friends. By your bedside as you (try to) sleep. Sure you can switch it off, or leave it behind, but it's a fierce temptation to resist.

HOUSEHOLD NAME

Finally, there is high-octane fame: national or worldwide celebrity. Topping the mainstream media charts. Selling out a stadium. Appearing on TV and in the movies, on red carpets and in gossip magazines.

In one way, this kind of fame is like a more intense version of the social media varieties—louder praise, more vicious criticism, bigger opportunities, larger checks, more outrageous demands, more threatening stalkers, and weirder weirdos. But there is also a different quality to this fame—it's more mediated, less direct than social media stardom. For one thing, it is filtered through mainstream media, such as TV, newspapers, or the movie industry, which move at a slower pace than social media. And for another, there are often intermediaries between you and your audience—agents, managers, producers, editors, hospitality staff, and security guards. You live in a world of insider politics. You need people you can trust around you, to help with the workload and act as a buffer.

Like living on a mountaintop, you gradually acclimatize to fame. Inevitably, it changes you. When I first meet someone who spends a lot of time in the public eye, I often sense that an invisible guard has been lowered provisionally, giving me a chance to relate to them as a person. If we go on to work together, the guard comes down for real; but this kind of trust has to be earned. Because the guard is necessary to protect them from the attention and demands of the public.

Here's another way to look at fame: your public persona is a mask—the word "persona" is Latin for the mask worn by an actor. The art of dealing with fame is the art of knowing when to wear the mask and play the part, and when to take it off. If you identify with the mask you're in big trouble, it is scrutinized so relentlessly and unforgivingly. But the people I've met who handle fame with the most grace and sanity can pick up the mask and play it masterfully, with heartstopping intensity. Then the next moment, they can put it down and be just someone sitting on a sofa, looking you candidly in the eye.

Reputation

In the opinion of some respected literary critics, Geoffrey Hill is the greatest living poet writing in English. Yet there's a fair chance you have never heard of him. He is the archetypal "poet's poet," better known and appreciated by his fellow practitioners than by the general public. Hill has a sense of humor about the situation—in one interview he responded to a question about his readership by saying that when he checked his royalty statements, he seemed not to have a readership.[1]

The artist Jack Vettriano has a very different relationship with critics and the public, exemplified by the fate of his best-known

---

1 For Geoffrey Hill's interview with the *Oxonian Review*, visit: OxonianReview.org/wp/geoffrey-hill

work, *The Singing Butler*. Rejected by the prestigious Royal Academy Summer Exhibition in 1992, the painting became the best selling art print in the UK, with the original fetching £744,800 at auction in 2005. A series of put-downs by critics and gallerists has done nothing to stem the enthusiasm of the public and collectors for his work, with the result that he is one of the best known and most commercially successful artists in the UK.

Hill and Vettriano illustrate the difference between fame and artistic or critical reputation: fame is a measure of the number of people who know your work, while reputation is an aggregate of the critical judgments of industry insiders, including practitioners, reviewers, academics, and awards panels. In the "high reputation, low fame" corner, we find arthouse movies, alternative rock bands, cult authors, and avant garde artists of all kinds. In the "low reputation, high fame" corner are the blockbusters, soap operas, talent contests, and romance novels that make their creators famous (and often rich) regardless of what the critics think.

Some people are happy with one or the other. No one in their right mind writes haiku because they want to be a household name, and no one enters *The X Factor* because they want broadsheet critics and university professors to write admiring articles about them.

A few creators manage to combine a stellar critical reputation with fame and fortune. Bob Dylan's music is known and loved worldwide, and critics have run out of superlatives to describe his artistic achievements. He even has professors writing papers and organizing symposia about his work. Quentin Tarantino has created several undisputed cinema classics, won two Oscars among many other awards, and generated over a billion dollars in box office revenue. Hilary Mantel's novels *Wolf Hall* and *Bringing Up the Bodies* have captured the popular imagination, become international bestsellers and been adapted for a BBC television series broadcast on both sides of the Atlantic, as well as a stage production by the Royal Shakespeare Company. Both novels won the prestigious Man Booker Prize, making her the only woman to have won the prize twice.

For some people, artistic reputation is nothing but snobbery. For others, fame is shallow and demeaning. But to dismiss one or the other is to miss the point. Both are very difficult to achieve, and require tremendous focus and dedication. Both are dangerously seductive—you can invest a lot of ego and waste a lot of time worrying about your reputation and/or fame. For your own sanity as well as your artistic integrity, you need to evaluate and validate your own work, regardless of what others think. But ego aside, both reputation and fame serve a practical function: *giving you access to the audience you want to reach.*

We have already seen that fame is essential to success in some fields, such as pop music or genre fiction, as your income is directly proportional to the number of sales you make. So there's a strong case for sidestepping traditional publishers and record labels, selling direct, and keeping the lion's share of the profits from your work.

But if you are working in a field such as fine art, poetry, or literary fiction, where reputation is highly prized and the enthusiasts are keenly aware of which platforms (galleries, publishers, journals, prizes) have the most prestige, then it's harder to sidestep the gatekeepers. I know artists who avoid selling art online because it will lower their status in the eyes of the collectors who frequent the top galleries. They command higher prices and make more money selling via a respected gallery. Many literary prizes, reviewers, and critics will not even consider self-published work; so writers who are more concerned with reputation than money or fame continue to submit their work to editors and agents.

Even in these more conservative creative fields, there are signs of change—some artists manage to maintain their status (and prices) while selling direct and one or two established poets have told me they are considering self-publishing their next book. But for now, those who want to build a reputation in such artistic fields still need to take account of the views of industry insiders.

Opportunity

Why are so many people prepared to work for little or nothing—making tea, running errands, ordering taxis, and doing the photocopying—on movie sets, in ad agencies, and in TV and fashion studios? Because it gives them a foot in the door, an opportunity to be in the right place when more exciting positions become available.

The dark side of opportunity is exploitation. There are countless stories of young creatives whose "internship" or "apprenticeship" turned out to be nothing more than a chance for their employer to get cheap or free labor without giving anything meaningful in return. But real opportunity is different: ultimately, it is the only reward worth having.

The story goes that The Smiths were born one afternoon when an enthusiastic Johnny Marr knocked on Morrissey's door and persuaded him to start writing songs together. If Marr had stayed at home that day, maybe someone else would have knocked and Morrissey would have teamed up with another guitarist. Or maybe neither of them would have found the right partner, and we would never have heard of either of them.

Like Marr, you have a choice: you can wait for opportunity to knock, or you can go out and find it yourself. Right now, as you read these words, there is someone somewhere with whom (or for whom) you could do great work. Your mission, if you choose to accept it, is to go out and find them.

If you look at the extrinsic rewards we have covered so far you can see that their greatest value lies in the fact *they can create opportunities for you.* Money, fame, and reputation are nice in themselves, but the pleasures they bring are short-lived. Money is soon spent. Someone else will be making the headlines tomorrow. There are only so many times you can replay a compliment in your mind. Laurels wither. Gold discs and Oscars gather dust.

So if you treat extrinsic rewards as a destination, you will end up dissatisfied and disillusioned, like Elvis in his mansion. But if you treat them as *tools to get things done*, you can use them to take your work and career to a whole new level. It's a whole lot easier to make things happen with funds and a good reputation: you can buy the best equipment and hire experts to help you; people know your name and want to work with you; customers are ready and waiting for your next release. Your last success means you can afford to dream bigger next time...

... And as you start to dream again, we have looped back into intrinsic motivation: **rewards become truly rewarding when you treat them as doorways to opportunity**. It works like the GO! square in Monopoly—each time you circle round you are a little wiser and (hopefully) richer, so you can build on a larger scale. Each time round brings new challenges, new fascinations, and a whole new set of opportunities.

106

EXTRINSIC MOTIVATION

Using rewards effectively

Here are some ways to ensure extrinsic motivation doesn't interfere
with your creativity, while claiming and enjoying your share of
the rewards on offer:

- **Don't sell yourself short**
- **Be bold**
- **The art of emotional pricing**
- **When to consider rewards**
- **Raise your profile**
- **Wear fame lightly**
- **Cultivate your reputation**

Don't sell yourself short

One of the biggest mistakes creatives make is agreeing to do something for little or no reward, because the project is intrinsically
attractive. Not that there is anything wrong with that if it's what
you really want—for example if you are financially comfortable
and want to donate your time and talent to a good cause. And
sometimes it makes sense to do work for fun, publicity, or other
reasons.

But if someone asks you to provide them with a professional
service—whether as a freelancer or employee—then tells you

they "don't have much budget" to pay you, you should stop and think carefully.

Are they really so poor? Or does the lack of budget simply indicate that they don't see this (or you) as a priority?

If they are not prepared to make much of a financial commitment to you, why should you make a big commitment of time and energy to them?

If they promise you "exposure" in return for your work, ask for details and examples of other creatives who have benefited from similar publicity. Unless they come up with concrete details, you should be suspicious.

And beware if they ask you to work for peanuts with vague promises of better-paid projects in the future. In my experience, clients, employers, and others who don't value your work at the start of a relationship never will.

Far too many creatives use the fact that they love the work so much as a reason for ducking negotiations and accepting a bad deal. We tell ourselves that this is because we are "just starting out," or that "it will be so much fun," or that the project "is a great opportunity" that could "lead to better things"—but actually it is a form of cowardice. We are afraid to step up and ask for what we are worth, or we feel so desperate for work that we take anything that comes along.

If you say "yes" to a deal like this, you start by breathing a sigh of relief: you have landed a new project. But as time passes, you find yourself working longer hours for less money, feeling stressed-out and resentful, and anything but inspired.

Over and over I have seen coaching clients reach a turning point in their career when they realize that, in the long run, it is *less* stressful to confront their fears, raise their prices, and walk away from unpromising engagements, than it is to deal with the consequences of under-charging and under-earning. The less stressed they are, the more energy and focus they have for their work.

So if you *really* want to do your best work and have a truly rewarding career, you need to:

- **Ditch the desperation**—learn to recognize this feeling, and never let it make the decision for you
- **Be selective**—decide on your criteria for the ideal client/project/job/opportunity (and a "minimum acceptable" if the ideal version is in short supply)
- **Know your true value**—and ask for it
- **Make your conditions clear**—let the other party know what they will need to do to work with you
- **Be prepared to walk away**—you are better off looking for something else than saying "yes" to a nightmare project

Be bold

When David came to me for coaching he was starting to feel burned out. He provided a very creative, very original, and very effective form of consultancy to a niche market in the creative industries. He had a great reputation, but his bank balance wasn't so spectacular.

"My clients rave about my work," he said, "so why am I always working, always exhausted, and always stressed about money?"

He had approached me when he found himself dragging his feet in responding to new business inquiries. Instead of feeling excited at the prospect of a new client, he saw it as just more work that was not worth the time and stress.

Our investigations revealed two big problems with his business: firstly, he was charging by the hour, and only selling a few hours at a time. Secondly, he was saying "yes" to every new business inquiry—customers were the lifeblood of his business, after all, and he had never even considered turning one down.

As a result he had lots of clients on short-term contracts, some of whom were not a good fit for his services. Apart from the long hours, it was mentally tiring to keep track of so many clients and their needs. And a small number of difficult clients took up so much of his time and caused so much stress that he never spent as much time as he would have liked with his favorite clients.

He was frustrated—not just on his own account, but because he knew there was more he could do for his clients, if only he had more time with them.

I knew how he felt, as I had been in a similar place with my own business a few years previously. I asked him the question my own coach, Peleg Top, had asked me at that time:

EXTRINSIC MOTIVATION

> "Supposing your ideal client came along and told you that money was no object: they would pay whatever it took to get your best work, so you could take all the time in the world to give them an amazing service. What kind of program would you create and deliver for this person?"

David went away for a few days, then came back with a description of an in-depth VIP program that would take several months to deliver and which was designed to effect a total transformation of a client's business. As he described it, he was more animated than I had ever seen him. Then he trailed off and looked concerned.

> "I'd need to charge a hell of a lot for this, wouldn't I?"
> "Too right!"
> "But will anyone pay it?"
> "Most people won't. But how many clients do you need at that price?"
> "Not many, I guess…" His enthusiasm was returning.

I asked David to go through his list of past clients and pick out his absolute favorites, the ones who valued his work the most and with whom he'd love to work again. He then approached each one with a personalized invitation to be one of the first to experience his new program.

The first client said it sounded amazing but he didn't have the budget. The second client said it sounded great, but he was too busy—maybe next year. By the time he got to the fourth client, David was starting to feel discouraged, but that was wiped out by elation when the client said "yes!"

Within a short time David had transformed his consultancy. Having previously averaged $5,000 a month, he made $25,000 within six weeks. And he was having the time of his working life: his newfound boldness meant the work was easier, he invested more of himself, and got more out as a result. He told me that his work now *gave* him energy, rather than *draining* it. With fewer clients, he finally had the time to devote his full care and attention to each of them, so he was doing the best work of his career. His clients loved it.

The change was dramatic, but it was not a miracle. David had a lot going for him—skills, experience, dedication, and genuine care for his clients. He also had a good reputation and network. The one thing he lacked was the boldness to create an outsize program that delivered outsize results. He also learned to be bolder in defining his ideal client, actually turning down inquiries from prospects who didn't fit the profile.

If you are an experienced creative working too hard for too little, in spite of having customers and/or fans who love your work, maybe boldness is the missing ingredient for your success. Here are some questions to help you find out.

IF YOU ARE SELF-EMPLOYED:

1. What is your average sale?

2. Supposing you added a zero to that price, and someone paid it. What is the most amazing thing (artwork, artefact, consulting program, etc.) you could create for that person?

3. Why not create that and make it your business to find the person who will happily pay for it?

IF YOU ARE EMPLOYED:

1. What is your current salary?

2. Supposing your boss offered you a 50 per cent pay raise on condition you came up with a way to add 50 per cent more value to the company. What would you come up with?

3. Why not come up with that right now, and make it your business to demonstrate so much value to an employer (maybe your current one) that they will happily pay you that?

The art of emotional pricing

"How much should I charge?"

I hear this question a lot from creatives wrestling with the perennial question of how much a unique piece of art, or a stylish design, or an engrossing story, or a transformational creative service is worth in hard cash.

There are many answers to this question, and several well-known methods for working out your prices, such as benchmarking against your competitors; or deciding how much you want to earn in a year and dividing that by the number of sales you expect to make; or calculating and demonstrating the value of the work to your buyer. Sometimes I'll use one or more of these methods to help my client work out their fees.

But with a particular type of client I give a different answer:

"I think you already know."

My hunch is that when you have amazing work for sale, a certain level of experience, and reasonable knowledge of your market, then at some level you know the value of your work— even if you may be afraid to say the number out loud to a customer. In this case, instead of working out their price, I suggest they *feel* it out.

I start deliberately low. For example, if I'm working with an artist:

Me: "Just imagine you've sold this painting for $50. How do you feel?"

Client: "Like I want to vomit."

Me: "OK, so $50 equals vomiting. Now imagine you've sold it for $250. How does that feel?"

Client: "Well, a bit better I suppose."

Me: "Right. $250 equals 'a bit better I suppose.' Now imagine you've sold it for $500."

Client: "OK I could be happy with that…"

We keep going up the scale, raising the price and checking in with their feelings (and ignoring doubts)—from feeling terrible, to feeling OK, to happy, to excited, to excited-and-a-bit-scared,

113

CHAPTER 11   USING REWARDS EFFECTIVELY

to feeling really scared. This gives us a beautifully calibrated **emotional pricing scale**, with prices linked to feelings.

Then I ask how they want to feel after the sale. They nearly always pick "excited-and-a-bit-scared." Which gives them a price—which is nearly always higher than the one they usually charge.

Sometimes they hesitate. They know the number they want, but are afraid of looking "greedy" or "arrogant." One way to help them past this is to focus on a certain competitor who charges in this range, and ask whether they consider their own work to be inferior to the competitor. If they answer a strong "No!" they usually realize fear is the only thing holding them back—then resolve to be brave.

Sometimes I ask them to put themselves in their buyer's shoes and imagine whom they'd rather do business with: a creator who feels disappointed and resentful about the deal or a creator who is as pleased as they are with the outcome?

It also helps to focus on how the buyer will feel when they experience the work: when you are agonizing over your prices, it's easy to forget that we all feel great when we buy something amazing.

If you're an experienced creative struggling financially while getting feedback that you are under-charging, here's how to start using emotional pricing.

Important. Emotional pricing is not for beginners. It requires a certain level of creative accomplishment, as well as knowledge of your market. And it does not apply to mass markets, such as ebooks, apps, or digital music downloads where you can often make more money by lowering your prices and selling more units. In these markets, it's often wiser to *ignore* how you feel about the price of an individual unit—it may feel "unfair" to charge only $3.99 for an ebook that took you months to write. Your time, effort, and creativity are worth a lot more than that. But you will sell *far* more copies at $3.99 than $20, so when the money rolls in, you should feel better at a lower price point.

Emotional pricing works best for creatives who are selling "originals"—artworks or creative services. Start by checking whether emotional pricing is appropriate for your situation.

- Are you confident that you are creating high-quality work?
- Are you getting feedback—from customers, peers, and/or mentors—that your work is of a high standard?
- Do you have a basic knowledge of what constitutes low, average, and high fees in your market? (Emotional pricing isn't "charge what you like"—to calibrate your scale, you need some connection with actual prices being paid for comparable work.)
- Are you earning significantly less than you want to for the hours and effort you put in?
- Do you ever find it hard to motivate yourself to work because you feel you are not being adequately rewarded for it?
- Do you find yourself envying competitors who earn more than you, when you believe your work is at least as good as theirs?

If you answer "yes" to at least half these questions, here's how to use emotional pricing for your creative work:

1. Pick an absurdly low price, and then imagine you have just sold your work (painting, print, project) for that price.

2. Ignore any thoughts that arise and focus on your body: how does it feel? What emotions do you experience? At this price point, you should be feeling pretty bad! So don't stay here long. Write down the price, and the feeling next to it, and move on.

3. Now move the price up a little and repeat steps 1–2. Notice the difference in how you feel. At this stage you should feel less bad, if not exactly great.

4. Keep raising the price and repeating steps 1–2 until you have gone through a range of positive feelings, to a point where the price is so high it feels really scary or plain ridiculous.

5. Now you have your **emotional pricing** scale. Look at it, and decide how you want to feel after a sale. I recommend the point where you feel fantastic plus a twinge of fear.

6. If you're hesitating about actually charging the price you picked at step 5, consider one of your competitors whose prices are in this range. Is their work so much better than yours? If not, then only fear is holding you back. Time to be brave!

7. If you're still hesitating, look at it from the buyer's point of view, and ask what kind of person you want to buy from: someone who feels disappointed and unmotivated? Or as pleased as you with the transaction? This is particularly important if you are selling a service, since as a buyer you will naturally want to have a motivated and enthusiastic professional at your service.

When to consider rewards

If you are a creative professional, you need to find a way to juggle intrinsic and extrinsic motivations. One way to do this for creative projects—whether jobs, freelance gigs, or your own artworks or products—is to divide them into **Before**, **During**, and **After** stages, and focus on different motivations at each stage:

1. BEFORE YOU START
Consider the work itself (intrinsic).

- Does it inspire you?
- Will it be enjoyable?

- Will you enjoy working with the people involved?

Consider the rewards on offer (extrinsic).

- Will it be financially worthwhile?
- Will it bring significant and relevant publicity?
- Will it enhance your reputation within your field?
- How likely is it to lead to other opportunities?
- Is there a deal-breaker in there?

Never agree to take on a project unless you are convinced that it fits one of these four scenarios.

- **An Ideal Project**—You are excited about the work itself, as well as the rewards (high intrinsic, high extrinsic).
- **A Labor of Love**—You are so excited about the work itself that you are genuinely not bothered about money or other rewards (high intrinsic, low extrinsic).
- **A Money Gig**— The work is not very inspiring, but the rewards (financial or otherwise) are so great you don't mind doing it (low intrinsic, high extrinsic).
- **A Minimum Viable Project (MVP)**—It's not the most exciting work, nor the best rewarded but the rewards will make it worthwhile and the other party agrees to your terms (minimum intrinsic, minimum extrinsic).

2. DURING THE PROJECT
Forget the rewards: focus 100 per cent on the work.

3. AFTERWARDS
Review the work.

- Did you enjoy it?
- Are you proud of it?

Review the rewards.

- Did you get what you were promised?
- Did the rewards make it worth your while?

Finally ...

- What will you do differently next time?

Raise your profile

If you want to become better known and start attracting opportunities you need to reach out and touch a lot of lives—to entertain, inspire, and/or help them.

Here are some principles for attracting the right kind of audience for your work. Marketing and promotion are huge subjects, so here I will focus on the fundamentals, and help you avoid some of the classic mistakes made by creatives.

DO YOU NEED TO BE "IN THE MEDIA"?

I sometimes talk to creators who are desperate to "get a break" by being picked up by big media—TV, radio, newspapers, or magazines. They seem to think being featured in what we used to call "the media" will catapult them to success and solve all their problems. Believe me, it probably won't.

My own work has been featured in national magazines and newspapers on both sides of the Atlantic, including the *Wall Street Journal*, *Vogue US*, and *Creative Review*. When I was a psychotherapist, the Discovery Health Channel broadcast a 30-minute documentary about my work. All of these things were fun to do. Friends and clients told me they were impressed. Some of the features brought a flurry of new business inquiries. But all of them together have not made a fraction of the difference to my business that my own online promotion has. When I talk to friends and clients, I hear the same story: a TV or magazine feature is good for the ego, and can make a good impression on others, but it rarely boosts sales or makes a big difference to their careers. Creatives who pin their hopes on being "discovered" are setting themselves up for disappointment.

The main exceptions are people who *work* in traditional media—such as journalists, actors, models, TV and radio presenters: they need to be seen "in the media" because it makes them visible to influential gatekeepers. If that's you, then you will need industry-specific advice about the best media strategy for your career. Even with this, you will likely also want to grow your online audience to capitalize on your media profile and help you launch your own projects.

So unless you work in traditional media, I recommend you focus most of your efforts on attracting an audience online—because that's where you have the most creative control and where your efforts are likely to result in the most impact. No, you won't become a household name overnight, but you can build a growing awareness of your work over time—maybe slowly, but also steadily and creatively.

THE CORNERSTONES OF YOUR PUBLIC PROFILE
These are the four foundations of your online profile:

1. **Identity**—Whom do you want to connect with? Who are you for this audience? Why should they care?
2. **Presence**—Where will you show up to connect with your audience?
3. **Media**—What media will you create? Will you give it away or charge for it?

4. Sharing —How will you distribute your media and communicate with your audience?

The first two are about making decisions and setting up your platform(s). The fourth can be largely automated. So long term, you will focus most of your efforts on number three: creating extraordinary media content.

1. IDENTITY

This is about the relationship between you and your audience.

Whom do you want to connect with?

"Anyone" and "everyone" are the wrong answers. If something is for everyone, it's for no one. Think about your favorite band when you were a teenager. What kind of people liked this band? What kind of people hated it? Notice how the love and hate were two sides of the same coin: people were *passionate* about them because they stood for something, and they weren't for everyone. In fact, there was *no band* everyone liked, was there?

So who is your ideal audience?

Your work may be designed for a very specific audience, such as Young Adult fiction or websites for artists. In which case you have a clear idea of who you want to reach. Traditional marketers define their audience in terms of categories such as age, gender, income, location, family size, social class. If you know this about your audience, it can help—but don't freak out if not.

For a lot of creative work, the critical factor that defines an audience is not an external characteristic such as their age or occupation, but an inner quality: *taste*. People's taste—in music, clothes, books, art, movies, and other entertainment—often transcends the boundaries of age, gender, nationality, or whatever. If that band is still going, pop along to a gig and you'll likely see all kinds of people in the crowd, but they will be connected by a common vibe.

So however else you define your audience, make it your mission to connect with people who share your taste. Each time you make a marketing decision—whether it's a design for your website, a name for your podcast, or what to say in your newsletter—choose something that matches that taste.

Who are you for this audience?

It's all well and good to say "myself"—but which self? In his classic book *The Presentation of Self in Everyday Life*, sociologist Erving Goffman argued that *all* encounters with other people are a performance in which we try to present those aspects of our self that are most appropriate to the situation. You present different aspects of yourself to your friends, your parents, your partner, your children, your colleagues—so why should your audience be any different?

Think about situations where you are called upon to show up in your professional role, such as a singer on stage, an architect on the building site, a designer meeting a client, or a writer giving an interview. Maybe you have just had an argument with your partner, or your car has broken down. Whatever, you need to put it aside and "get into character." You aren't being "inauthentic," you are just setting aside one aspect of yourself while you express another one. You do this unconsciously every day—the challenge is to do it more consciously and artfully when you present yourself in the public eye.

How can you know which aspects of yourself and your work will be most compelling for your audience? One way is to notice what has already grabbed your audience's attention. Even if you only have a handful of readers, clients, or listeners, you have probably heard them tell you what they like about your work. (If not, ask them!) Pay particular attention when you hear the same comments over and over from different people.

This is not just an artificial exercise to come up with a clever marketing image—when people describe what they love about you and your work, they are describing the bigger you—someone who is wiser and more powerful than the everyday you.

2. PRESENCE

The center of your online world should be **your website**—Your-Name.com or YourBrandName.com. This is where people go to learn about you, buy from you, contact you, and subscribe to your mailing list (see **Sharing** below).

Your website does not need to be elaborate or expensive. At Wordpress.org (not Wordpress.com) you can download free software for building a website or fully-functioning blog; you can then hire a designer to create a unique design, or buy a pre-designed Wordpress theme. Another option for creating a beautiful portfolio website is ProSite.com from Behance.

Once your site is established, you can complement it by establishing a presence at other locations online:

- **Social networks**—to connect with your audience, network, and share your media content
- **Portfolio sites**—to showcase your creative work (e.g. Behance. net, DeviantArt.com)
- **Media platforms**—to distribute your media to wider audiences (e.g. iTunes for podcasts, YouTube for video, SoundCloud for audio)
- **Marketplaces**—to sell your work (e.g. Amazon, iTunes, Audible, Etsy)
- **Forums**—to debate and network with people who share your interests
- **Other people's blogs and podcasts**—as a guest author, host, or interviewee to reach their (sometimes very large!) audiences

You can't be everywhere. Decide on your goals (e.g. sharing your music, selling your books, connecting with fans, networking with peers) and focus on the smallest number of locations that will enable you to achieve them.

3. MEDIA

Think of yourself as the owner of a global media company. Your main "channel" is your own website—using Wordpress you can publish articles, images, audio, and video, as well as syndicate your media to subscribers via RSS and email.[1] But what kind of media should you create?

For some creative fields—such as writing fiction or developing apps—your best marketing content is the product itself. Customers for these products are used to shopping for them on dynamic marketplaces (Amazon, iBookstore, the App Store, etc.) with powerful search, recommendation, and review systems. So your best bet is to increase your visibility within the stores by creating more products.

If you are selling physical artworks or products, or tickets to live performances, you can't simply upload these to your website! So as well as doing your work, you need to create separate **marketing media**. Even if you are creating digital content to sell in online stores, it may well be worthwhile creating marketing media. For example, many nonfiction authors blog or podcast about their field of expertise to raise awareness of their books.

The lines between art and marketing can get very blurred. For example, a singer sells tickets for live performances and sells CDs at each show. She films the show and posts video excerpts on her blog, YouTube, and Facebook as marketing media. She also shares excerpts from her album on Soundcloud and sells the album via iTunes and other stores.

---

1 Aweber.com and MailChimp.com are two good options for setting up an email subscription to your blog, so that every post is automatically emailed out to your subscribers. Search their help sections for "RSS to email" for instructions on setting this up.

What kind of marketing media should you create? Obviously not just sales messages—that's boring for you and annoying for your audience. You can be more imaginative than that. Here are a few options.

- **Artwork/product photos**—essential for any kind of physical artwork or product
- **Demonstration videos**—explaining how to use your products
- **Performance videos**—capturing your live shows
- **Free samples**—such as a chapter from your book, a song from your album, or the first module of your training course
- **Entertainment**—stand alone comedy videos, demo songs, short stories, amusing articles, etc.
- **Education**—teaching knowledge or skills that are related to your products or services
- **Thought pieces**—expressing your opinion on important subjects related to your field
- **Back story**—revealing your sources of inspiration, working methods, or aspects of your personal life
- **Critiques**—reviewing or analyzing the work of your creative heroes or peers (a great way to demonstrate your expertise without talking about yourself directly)
- **Interviews**—giving interviews to bloggers and podcasters, or interviewing others on your own platform

Before you commit yourself, study the media landscape of your industry, to see what gaps you can spot in the thinking, or the types of media available to enthusiasts. Are there lots of magazines but not many quality podcasts? Do all the blogs take the same angle? Which people or points of view are under-represented? What can you create that will make a refreshing change?

Play to your strengths and follow your inclinations—if you hate writing but love talking, a podcast makes more sense than a blog.

Don't feel pressured to publish every day or even every week—better to publish something amazing once or twice a month than something mediocre twice a week. Whatever media you create, you need to write a title and description that entices people to engage with it—so you need to learn some basic copywriting skills.[2]

4. SHARING

There's no point creating amazing media unless you can transmit it to your audience—not just once, but each time you have something new to say or share. Here are three of the most common options for sharing, in order of their typical effectiveness.

Email subscriptions

People subscribe directly to your mailing list by entering their email address into your email marketing system (e.g. Aweber.com, MailChimp.com). This is the most powerful means of sharing for two reasons: firstly, most people check their email every day, so they are likely to see every email you send them; secondly, you have their email addresses so you can take your list with you if you switch providers.

Mediated subscriptions

People subscribe to your content via an intermediate service *without* giving you their contact details (e.g. subscribing to your podcast via iTunes, to your blog via Feedly, or to your video channel via YouTube). This is less powerful than email subscription, as not everyone checks their podcast app or Feedly reader every day, and also because you do not have their contact details—if you switch provider, you lose your subscribers.

---

2 CopyBlogger.com is a good place to start learning about online copywriting. Begin with the guide to writing magnetic headlines: www.copyblogger.com/magnetic-headlines

Social networks

Every time someone connects with you on a social network, they are effectively subscribing to receive updates from you. But remember, the primary purpose of social networks is *socializing*. People will unfollow fast if you just send out sales messages. Secondly, we do *not* see every update published on our networks! So the chance of people seeing your messages is much lower than via email. Finally you don't have their contact details, so if you leave the network, you lose touch with them.

Important *Effective sharing requires permission.* Never add someone to your email list without asking their permission! You've doubtless had people add you to their list without asking, so you know how annoying this is. Apart from politeness, it's much more effective to contact people who have *actively chosen* to receive your emails. That's why Seth Godin describes mailing lists as "permission assets"—the list becomes a powerful asset only when you earn your audience's permission to contact them.

Building momentum

Once you have done the hard thinking about your identity, decided where to focus your online presence, and set up your automated subscription, one of your main ongoing promotional tasks will be producing and publishing high-quality creative media. Which should be good news for a creative professional!

You won't become an overnight success, and you may never be a household name. But if you do this right, you will become better and better known to the kind of people you want to inspire, entertain, and/or help—enough to sustain your business or reach your career goals. More than that, you have the opportunity to touch a lot of people's lives and make your mark.

Wear fame lightly

Whether you're on worldwide TV or you've just attracted your first 100 Twitter followers, fame can be a heady cocktail. Here are some tips for avoiding intoxication and a nasty hangover.

ENJOY THE LIMELIGHT

If you've made an effort to get your work and your name out there in public, then enjoy the times when you succeed. This may be easier if you are a natural extrovert, but—speaking as a lifelong introvert—it's possible for anyone to enjoy an audience's appreciation, even if it takes a little time to get used to it.

Don't pretend you're not flattered by the attention. Enjoy it for what it is—and don't take it too seriously. Tomorrow those people will be singing someone else's praises. So let them go. They'll be back, if you create something amazing for them to come back to.

SPEND PLENTY OF TIME OFF STAGE

Japanese *kabuki* actors spend more time on stage than most performers, giving several shows a day for large chunks of the year. There are stories of veteran actors losing touch with everyday reality—they spend so long in makeup and in character that it becomes a moot point whether the actor or the role is the "real" person.

If that sounds exotic and extreme, consider the effect of spending all day every day (and some of the night) plugged into social media on your smartphone, playing your public persona (mask). Yes, your professional persona is closer to the everyday you than a male kabuki star is to his role as a medieval princess, but remember Erving Goffman: *every* encounter with other people is a performance, and every performance involves effort and constriction, however subtle. So make sure you spend plenty of time each day "off stage"—whether that means moving away from the hotel balcony and closing the window to drown out the screams from the adoring crowd below, or switching off Twitter for a couple of hours before bed. (Obviously, you never Tweet in bed. Do you?)

Exercise, meditation, massage, and hot baths are excellent ways to leave the mask behind, by reconnecting with your body and calming your mind through present-moment awareness. Another good option is to lose yourself in another world—a good novel, movie, or TV drama.

Extroverts: this includes you too! Just as it's good for us introverts to get used to the limelight, so you can benefit from getting comfortable with your own company.

KEEP PRACTICING YOUR ART

Fame is a side effect of your work, not its purpose. The best reminder of this is daily practice of your art. You are grounded by the sight of your workspace, the feel of your familiar tools, and the smell of paint, incense, coffee, or whatever else you associate with that place.

Fame is like the weather—or at least the weather here in Britain: sometimes delightful, sometimes disappointing, always unpredictable. But whatever is happening in the world outside, you can rely on your creative work. After a glowing review of your latest work, nothing brings you down to earth like getting stuck in a tricky part of the next one. After a scathing public attack or spectacular failure, nothing will console you like getting into the flow of a new composition. Crowds may come and go, but you will always have your work to turn to.

CHERISH PEOPLE WHO DON'T BELIEVE THE HYPE

One of the biggest challenges for well-known people is being surrounded by people who relate to them purely as their public persona. Gushing praise is nicer than biting criticism, but it's the emotional equivalent of ice cream—nice as a treat, not so good as a staple diet. So make sure you spend plenty of time with people who don't believe the hype about you (positive or negative) and who relate to you as a human being.

In your personal life, this means making time for the people who love you for who you are outside your professional role, whether family or close friends. The people who let you be yourself and who tease you affectionately about your other life as a rock star, fashion icon, and/or immortal genius. Don't worry so much about the ones who carp at your success or say "you've changed," as if it were a criticism. Of *course* fame changes you. Life changes all of us, all the time. Cherish the people who respect and celebrate the creative changes you are making in your life—and make sure you do the same for them.

Professionally, beware of surrounding yourself with yes-men and -women. Get help and advice from people who aren't afraid to challenge you when they think it's in your best interests. Remember the kings and queens who were wise enough to keep an "all-licensed fool" in their court, given permission to prick the bubble of self-importance with jokes at their expense. Personally, I like getting help from people who are used to working with people who are more successful than I am. For one thing, they are really good at what they do. And for another, their client list reminds me that I'm far from the most impressive person they will deal with this week.

Cultivate your reputation

Cultivating your artistic or critical reputation is about ensuring that enthusiasts and influencers within your field know and respect your work.

In some creative fields—such as genre fiction or rock music—this kind of reputation is becoming less and less important, since the audience is more interested in the work than who publishes it or what the critics think of it. And the creators are more focused on reaching their public than garnering awards and broadsheet reviews. They sell direct to their audience and are more than happy with fame and fortune.

In more conservative fields, such as fine art, literary fiction, or classical music, the audience is more likely to be impressed by the reputation of the gallery, publisher, or record label that presents the work. So if you want to reach these people, you may have to play the game of influencing the "right" people and having your work appear in the "right" places. If you are in this position, here are some tips on playing the game to win—as well as with style, sportsmanship, and pleasure.

CULTIVATE, DON'T OBSESS

Obviously, the foundation of a great artistic reputation is great art. There are no short cuts to this—you need to do the work, and do it sincerely. But you can't rely on producing your masterpieces and waiting to be "discovered." You also need to artfully position your work—by having it published, exhibited, or performed in prestigious publications, galleries, or arenas.

Plenty of artists and creatives claim they never consider their reputation, but I take that with a pinch of salt. Reputations don't just happen—in almost all cases, they are carefully cultivated. However, cultivation is not a full-time job. When you cultivate a house plant, you need to give it regular care, watering, pruning, and maybe special plant food. But the plant won't grow any faster if you water it several times a day—you're more likely to kill it!

It's the same with your artistic reputation—the more you obsess about it, and obsessively promote yourself, the less time and attention you are devoting to your real work. And the more desperate and needy you come across to the people you want to impress.

GET TO KNOW THE SCENE

Start by getting to know the cultural scene where you want to make an impact. This could be as simple as asking around to find out which bars in town feature the best local bands or as complex as getting to know the leading artists, critics, galleries, and journals of the international contemporary art scene.

Make it your business to know who or what are the best-regarded names in each of the following categories:

- **Artists**
- **Influencers**—gallerists, editors, producers, critics, reviewers, bloggers, and heads of organizations
- **Venues**—arenas, galleries, conferences, bars, districts, online forums, social networks
- **Media**—TV and radio shows, journals, books, blogs, podcasts
- **Organizations**—publishers, galleries, studios, agencies, societies, colleges
- **Awards**

This shouldn't feel like work. If you are passionate about your creative discipline, you probably know a lot of this already, and finding out more will feel like fun. If it doesn't, ask yourself whether this is a scene you *really* want to belong to.

HANG OUT AND HELP OUT

It's amazing how many connections and opportunities emerge from spending time with others who share your enthusiasm. Often an opportunity arises when you least expect it. The crucial thing is that you show up, take part, and look for opportunities to help out.

Years ago I attended a poetry workshop and did my usual thing of joining in the discussion. The class happened to include one of the editors of the prestigious magazine *Magma Poetry*, which happened to be on the lookout for new poetry reviewers. The editor liked what she heard from me and mentioned my name to the *Magma* reviews editor—a few days later, I was invited to write a review for the next issue. Over the next few months I wrote several reviews and was then invited to join the editorial board and help produce and promote the magazine. That led to me editing an issue of the magazine—I found myself commissioning poems and interviews from famous poets, as well as making my own selection from the thousands of poems submitted.[1]

WORK WITH A MENTOR

Mentors are experienced practitioners and/or influencers, who give aspiring stars the benefit of their experience via formal tuition or informal advice. For industry-specific knowledge and strategies, it's hard to beat a good mentor. Some of them will introduce you to other influencers; others will expect you to create your own opportunities, albeit with their guidance.

How do you find a mentor? Some of them teach classes or offer mentoring programs you can apply for. Others are not so easy to engage—you have to be introduced or impress them with your work before they decide to take you under their wing. Mentoring often develops as an informal relationship, so finding one is not a step-by-step process. However there are things you can do to make yourself an appealing person to mentor, which can tip the odds in your favor.

- **Do your research**—look for potential mentors, learn everything you can about their work, and show up at their public

EXTRINSIC MOTIVATION

---

1 You can read issue 34 of *Magma Poetry*, which I edited, on the website of the UK Poetry Library via this link: LateralAction.com/magma34

appearances, where you may have an opportunity to speak to them.

- **Help them**—if they are speaking or teaching, bring friends and ask questions; if they publish online, respond with insightful comments, and share their content; email and ask if there's anything you can do to help.
- **Do your own thing**—mentors love to help people who are taking initiative and making things happen, without waiting for help.
- **Start small**—if you are in conversation, don't ask them to "mentor" you; ask for advice on a specific decision or task
- **Give feedback**—mentors love to know if they are making a difference, so if they give you advice, act on it and let them know the outcome.

APPLY FOR OPPORTUNITIES

Whatever your creative field, there will likely be established routes to success:

- Approaching galleries, record companies, publishers, producers, or agents
- Submitting to journals
- Entering competitions
- Auditioning for shows

The good news is that there are usually plenty of such opportunities available, and the gatekeepers are actively encouraging you to apply. There are usually deadlines for applications and responses, so you are left in no doubt of whether or not you are succeeding.

The bad news, of course, is that competition is high. You also adopt the posture of a supplicant, awaiting other people's judgment on your work, which doesn't feel good if you sustain it for too long. So you might want to combine this approach with creating your own platform and opportunities (see below).

Here are some tips for making the process more efficient and less painful:

- **Do your research.** Make sure you are targeting the right people—i.e. the ones who accept and promote your kind of work—otherwise you are wasting your time and theirs. Read their publications, go to their shows, investigate their back catalogue.
- **Find out how they like to be approached.** Some agents welcome submissions, others actively discourage them. There is an etiquette to approaching gallerists. Most publishers make their submissions guidelines clear.
- **Have a system.** Don't put all your eggs in one basket. Apply for as many relevant opportunities as you can find. When you are rejected from one place, move to the next on your list.
- **Get used to rejection!** It's normal. In fact, rejection and criticism are so common in the creative industries, I wrote a whole book—*Resilience*—about how to handle them.

BECOME A THOUGHT LEADER

The most effective way to influence your field is to become a thought leader yourself. This should happen naturally as you put out high quality work over time. You can amplify the process by writing thought pieces in leading journals, speaking at events, joining debates, and/or campaigning for important issues.

Another option is to create your own platform for sharing your work, communicating your ideas, and hosting discussions. These days there are plenty of options for doing this, including blogging, podcasting, YouTube channels, and social media networks. (See "Raise your profile" in this chapter for advice on doing this.) As your platform grows, people will start to approach *you* with proposals and opportunities. In some creative fields—such as book publishing or rock music—an established online platform is rapidly becoming a *requirement* for landing a publishing or recording deal. Since I started blogging and publishing my own books, I have been approached by several publishers, including Mann, Ivanov, and Ferber in Moscow, who now publish the Russian edition of my book *Resilience*.

While 21st century technology makes platform-building easier than ever, the principle is nothing new: back in 1922, T.S. Eliot founded the *Criterion*, a literary journal that became enormously influential and helped to cement his position as the pre-eminent poet of his age.

PERSONAL MOTIVATION

Your Values

138

CHAPTER 12

Staying true to yourself

"Better to fail in your own destiny than succeed in
  someone else's."
  The Bhaghavad Gita

On a warm spring night in 1993, the clouds part over the Old
Quad of Brasenose College, Oxford University; the lawn and 16th
century stone turn blue-silver in the moonlight.

A light is on in the northwest corner of the quad. Through
the window, you can see me sitting at my desk. This afternoon,
after weeks of intensive work, I handed in my dissertation. I have
promised myself the evening off as a reward, but I am acutely aware
that my final exams are only a few weeks away. After three years
as an undergraduate, I am entering the last stretch. *If I do some
revision tonight*, I tell myself, *I can get a head start for tomorrow.*
So I open a book and start to read.

But something is wrong.

As I try to focus, I feel my eyes screwing up with pain—the
familiar "tired eyes" I have experienced off and on for years. It's
particularly bad tonight, so I go to my bathroom and splash water on my eyelids. But the relief lasts only a minute or two, then
the eyes tense up again and my head starts to ache. It has never
been this bad before. *I guess I must be tired. I'll feel better in the
morning.* Reluctantly, I put the book down.

Next day I'm one of the first at breakfast in the college hall. As I hurry back to my room, the sunlight feels uncomfortably bright. Back at my desk I make a nasty discovery: my eyes are even worse than last night! The eyestrain and headache are coming on already, before I can read a single page, even after a full night's sleep. *What's wrong with me? I can't afford to lose any time!*

I start to panic.

All that day, and for days afterward, I fight a losing battle. Cold water, painkillers, drawn curtains, sunglasses, rest—nothing makes the slightest difference to the pain in my eyes. I *absolutely must* get on with my revision, because I am falling further behind every day. And I *absolutely cannot* read a single page of text. Each time I try, the pain is excruciating.

I am furious. This is the culmination of years of study: as a state school student, applying to Oxford felt like a big leap, and I was thrilled to land a place. But getting here was not enough: I wanted to be the best of the best, and felt I was on course when I achieved a First in my first year exams. Now here I am in the city of books, on the verge of my crowning success—and I can't read a single sentence. It is maddening.

Why am I so set on a First Class degree? At the start, it was pure ambition—the target was there, I found myself hitting it regularly in my weekly essays, so why not do the best I could? Now in the final year, when we are all considering our futures, I listen without interest as my friends discuss careers in law, medicine, the City, the press, and the Big Five accounting firms. I want to be a writer, and the idea of the corporate world fills me with horror.

So I set my sights on a Ph.D to give me a few more years of reading and writing. But funding is tight for English Ph.Ds. I am told "A First isn't enough, even from Oxford—it needs to be a really good First to have any chance of getting a grant." It has come to feel like a matter of life and death: either succeed in retaining my academic status, or go out into the big bad world to work for a faceless corporation for the rest of my life.

I go to my doctor, terrified there is something seriously wrong. He listens kindly and refers me to an eye specialist for assessment. The specialist examines my eyes and reassures me that there is absolutely nothing wrong with them. I am not losing my sight. I leave his office both relieved and confused. *If there's nothing wrong with my eyes, why do they hurt so much? Why can't I read?*

After several weeks, I accept defeat and withdraw from the exams, travelling home to Devon in what feels like disgrace. For the next eight months I am unable to read a book, watch television, or do anything that requires visual concentration—even board games. I feed my addiction to books by listening to endless audiobooks. Later I will learn that this state is called depression, but for now it just feels like hell.

Eventually I find myself in an office off Harley Street in London, being examined by one of the top eye specialists in the country. *If he tells me there is nothing wrong with my eyes*, I say to myself, *I am going to scream.*

"Mr McGuinness, there is nothing wrong with your eyes. But there is something wrong. And that something is stress."

I am dumbfounded. How can mere *stress* account for the extreme physical pain I am in? I'm not making it up! But I am relieved that he seems to be taking my condition seriously. He urges me to consider counseling, and seems surprisingly confident it will relieve the pain.

When I return to my doctor with the diagnosis, he suggests I try hypnotherapy. Now I am intrigued. I have never been hypnotized before, and I will do anything to be cured.

And a miracle happens.

Three sessions of hypnotherapy are all it takes to bring an end to my eight-month nightmare: the pain subsides and *I can read again!* It feels like I have been let out of prison.

I go back to Oxford the following year and take a different approach to my exams. On doctor's orders, I only work during the day, spending my evenings playing pool in the common room. And I fail to get a First. My tutor tells me I got "as close as it's possible to get to a First without actually getting one." I'm disappointed, but it's not the end of the world. Academia seems very far away now. And I have a new interest: hypnosis.

My biggest "failure" turns out to be the key to my future career path, setting me on a road I would never otherwise have considered. My training as a hypnotherapist is an amazing journey of discovery—learning about myself, about the unconscious mind and the weird yet somehow wise symptoms it can create,[1] and how to help people change long-standing patterns that have been holding them back. Practicing therapy leads to coaching my fellow creatives, which eventually becomes a thriving business based on my creative passions.

So why did I have to go through all of that?

I got an idea into my head about success and obsessed about it to the point where I forced myself to work harder and harder. But in my heart, this wasn't what I wanted. I was a poet, not an academic. It turned out I was a healer and a helper, too. It took a traumatic event to remind me of what was truly important to me and set me on a more fulfilling path. The eyestrain and headaches were horrible to experience, but looking back I can see that they were my body's way of reminding me of my deepest **personal motivation**—my values.

---

1 My colleague Dr. John Eaton would say that my eyestrain was a communication from Bodymind—the sophisticated emotional intelligence of the body—alerting me to the need for change in my life. For more about Bodymind, visit ReverseTherapy.com

WHAT ARE VALUES?

Values are shorthand for the kind of things that matter to us. They are typically expressed as abstract nouns, such as **freedom**, **creativity**, or **integrity**. (For the sake of clarity, in this section values appear in bold type.) The specific choices and actions we make are expressions of our values.

For example, if Lisa spends as much time as possible in pleasing environments (countryside, picturesque towns) and surrounds herself with aesthetic objects (paintings, clothes, furniture etc.) we can say that **beauty** is one of her most important values. But her brother Jake may spend most of his time in the bustling, ugly city, without caring much about clothes and home decor, because **excitement** and **opportunity** are higher values for him than **beauty**.

Our values reflect our sense of what is important (and unimportant), desirable (and undesirable), and morally right (and wrong). When we think and act in alignment with our values, we feel confident, energized, and at ease with ourselves. Staying creative throughout your career is not just a case of working hard—it's about staying true to your own values, and not being distracted by other people's standards.

When we lose touch with our values, we feel conflicted, inauthentic, and in some cases we can even experience physical symptoms of dis-ease. At Oxford I was focusing obsessively on **achievement** (even **perfection**!) while neglecting values of **creativity** and **joy**. It was only when I reconnected with those values and started expressing them in my actions that my symptoms disappeared and my zest for life returned.

VALUES ARE RELATIVE

Most of us share the same values—but we do not value them all equally. Look at this list of seven values and you will probably agree that all of them are important:

- Adventure
- Beauty
- Compassion
- Harmony
- Justice
- Pleasure
- Power

If you are a typical creative, you might value **beauty** and **pleasure** more highly than **power**, and follow a very different career path than your friend who is climbing the management ladder at a large corporation. But not all creatives will have the same value system—each of us has our individual preferences and priorities.

VALUES CAN CHANGE

Although, as the name suggests, our personal values feel very much a part of us, the examples above show that they can in fact change over time. When I spend time with my children I am delighted by the carefree way they value **fun** over **responsibility**—even if this creates problems from time to time! As they grow older, especially if they become parents themselves, **responsibility** is likely to rise up their ladder of values (but I hope they retain their sense of **fun**). Another example of changing values is expressed in the often-repeated saying: "If you are not a liberal at twenty you have no heart, if you're not a conservative at forty, you have no head."[2]

Sometimes we change our values in response to a crisis—this is the basis of most compelling stories, ancient and modern. Like the Biblical Saul of Tarsus, whose persecution of the early Christians

---

2 These words are often attributed to Winston Churchill, but according to the Quote Investigator website, they did not originate with him. For an exhaustive analysis of possible sources, visit: QuoteInvestigator.com/2014/02/24/heart-head

ended in the dust of the road to Damascus. Reborn as Paul the Apostle, he memorably expressed his new hierarchy of values as "**faith, hope** and **charity** . . . but the greatest of these is **charity**." (King James Bible, bold formatting mine.)

WHAT'S THE DIFFERENCE BETWEEN PERSONAL VALUES AND INTRINSIC MOTIVATIONS?

At first glance these two types of motivation look very similar— they are both "inner" motivations, more psychological than tangible. And some qualities (such as freedom, love, or learning) can be seen as both intrinsic motivations and personal values.

For my purposes, the key distinction is that intrinsic motivations are typically associated with the *task* in hand, whereas values are associated with the *person* doing the task. Intrinsic motivations are more generic—they apply to many different types of task, whereas values are more personal and specific, defining what *this* person is motivated by, to the exclusion (or lower priority) of other values.

For example, an artist, an entrepreneur, and an activist spend their time doing different types of work. While engaged in their different tasks, they are all likely to experience the same intrinsic motivations we looked at in Chapter 6: freedom, challenge, learning, purpose, inspiration, creative flow, and obsession. Yet they choose their particular paths and activities because of their values: the artist places a high value on **beauty** and **self-expression**, the entrepreneur on **wealth** and **competition**, and the activist on **justice** and **sustainability**.

There is also an overlap between some personal values (such as **wealth** and **competition**) and extrinsic motivations (such as money and status). The important distinction here is that extrinsic motivations are *external, tangible rewards* (such as money, awards, or a promotion) whereas values are about the *inner, personal meaning* of the rewards. This is why a professional footballer can be unhappy with a contract offer of £100,000 a week if a team-mate is earning £120,000—it's not just about the money (extrinsic reward) but about the implication that he is *not as good* as the other player (value: **competition**).

CHAPTER 13

Types of personal motivation

This chapter describes seven personal values, to illustrate how values work, and how acting in alignment with your values is one of the most important things you can do to stay motivated over the long term.

- **Adventure**
- **Beauty**
- **Compassion**
- **Harmony**
- **Justice**
- **Pleasure**
- **Power**

This list is by no means exhaustive—such a list would contain hundreds of values. But these seven cover a wide spectrum of personal motivations, and the principles they illustrate apply to any other values.

Adventure

We think of adventures as taking place long ago and far away, in distant lands, imaginary worlds, or outer space. But if you have the spirit of **adventure** inside you, you can find plenty of quests, dragons, and treasure right here and now on planet Earth. People who value adventure are drawn to exciting, difficult, and dangerous challenges—not just for the potential rewards, but for the thrill of testing themselves against adversity, and learning what they are made of.

THE UPSIDE OF ADVENTURE

We all loved tales of adventure as children, and there was (and maybe still is) a part of us that longed to go on a quest ourselves—if only we were brave enough. Adventures are exciting! They bring purpose and meaning to life. An adventure is a chance to do something extraordinary, even heroic.

I've always thought of my work as an adventure, not just a career. My adventure has led me into many odd places.

I've explored the boundaries of my mind, on silent meditation retreats in Buddhist monasteries, and floating in a pitch-black isolation tank.

I've worked with therapists, coaches, and mentors, to face my fears and change long-standing patterns of thought and behavior.

I've learned all kinds of skills and knowledge, from hypnosis to family therapy, poetic versification to corporate sales, public speaking to intellectual property law, online marketing to transformational coaching.

I've coached clients on six continents, who have been engaged in all kinds of weird, wonderful, and inspiring work, from fine art to amazing products and services, and innovative business models. I have travelled to the desert of the Middle East, the snows of Scandinavia, and the bustle of American cities to work with clients and speak at conferences.

I've explored the new frontiers opened up by technology, and published my writings to thousands of readers worldwide via my blogs, courses, and now books.

While pursuing my adventure I have created and discarded professional identities, companies, business models, products, and services. I have a low boredom threshold, but I have been pursuing this adventure for twenty years, and it still feels like an exciting journey.

On the surface, your adventure won't look much like mine, but it will lead you to many wonderful places and discoveries—if you follow it. Of course, you may try to resist, but your adventurous spirit will keep calling you . . .

THE FLIPSIDE OF ADVENTURE

The old mapmakers weren't joking when they wrote "Here be dragons."[1] Adventures are *dangerous*. Which is why many people prefer to stay at home (and complain about their unfulfilling life). Explorers may not have met actual dragons, but read accounts of their journeys and you will learn about real-life struggles with sea monsters, pirates, typhoons, whirlpools, icebergs, scorching deserts, monsoons, ferocious animals, terrifying warriors, poisonous creepy-crawlies, malnutrition, starvation, and hideous diseases.

I recently read *Samurai William* by Giles Milton, about William Adams, the first Englishman to reach Japan (in 1600) and the only foreigner ever to be honored with the rank of samurai. His adventure brought him wealth, influence, and the friendship of Shogun Oda Nobunaga, the most powerful man in Japan. But along the way he also had to endure a two-year sea voyage, eat raw penguin straight off the bone, watch his comrades die of scurvy, fight with native islanders and Spanish sailors, and survive the storms and typhoons that wiped out most of his fleet. When he got to Japan he was imprisoned by the Japanese and plotted against by

---

1 Apparently they were more likely to write "Here be lions."

Portuguese Jesuits before he made an ally of the Shogun; once he had got that far, he still had to learn the Japanese language, adapt to Japanese customs, and deal with loneliness and separation from his wife and children.

Rest assured there are plenty of terrifying hazards waiting for you if you are brave or foolish enough to choose a life of adventure. My own adventure has given me plenty of sleepless nights—worrying about money, or terrified of what I had committed to doing the following day. I've had my share of disasters and near-shipwrecks. I have had to dig deep to find the courage to continue, and some days I still have to look for it.

Courage is not about being fearless, but about facing and overcoming the source of your fear—whether that is a dragon, a hurricane, an audience, a demanding client, or a blank page or canvas. It is also about facing up to your own cowardice—the times when you shied away from a challenge, or failed to speak up, or sold yourself short out of fear. But without courage, and the willingness to face your fears, you will never experience the joy of succeeding at something almost impossibly difficult or unbearably scary.

Beauty

I can hardly write a book about creativity without mentioning **beauty**. When we say a piece of work is beautiful, we mean we experience a refined pleasure in the way it looks (paintings, sculpture, drawings, design), the way it sounds (music, recited poetry), or the way it stimulates our minds (stories, poetry). Beauty can be sensuous, or mental, or both, and it evokes powerful emotions—of delight, wonder, and even awe.

THE UPSIDE OF BEAUTY

I like to wake up in the morning and see the sun rising over the fields behind our home: it is beautiful. Some mornings I merely glance at it while I'm making breakfast, but other times it stops me in my tracks, the beauty is so intense and feels so significant. It uplifts my soul.

This is neither a new sensation nor a new idea: ancient Greek philosophers argued that it is through the experience of beauty that we apprehend the harmony of the universe. Aristotle even linked beauty to ethics, saying that "virtue aims at the beautiful" (*Nicomachean Ethics*). The idea that beauty is a key to knowledge is famously expressed by John Keats in his "Ode on a Grecian Urn":

> When old age shall this generation waste,
>   Thou shalt remain, in midst of other woe
> Than ours, a friend to man, to whom thou say'st,
>   'Beauty is truth, truth beauty,'—that is all
>   Ye know on earth, and all ye need to know.

On the one hand, a skeptic could argue that the beauty of Keats' verse gives his words undue weight: just because they *sound* delightful and authoritative does not make their argument logically true. Yet Keats might respond that the beauty of the words reinforces their logic: the *reason* they sound beautiful is that they are true, and vice versa.

If you value beauty, you choose your clothes and the furnishings of your home with care. Maybe you live in a particularly beautiful environment, even if it is not the cheapest part of town or the most convenient location in the countryside. You wince at the thought of having to live somewhere ugly, wear ugly clothes, or hang an ugly picture on your wall. Creating something beautiful is one of your main motivations for your work. Beauty is one of your chief criteria when evaluating creative work—whether your own or someone else's. Artists who deliberately create ugly art seem perverse and second-rate to you.

THE FLIPSIDE OF BEAUTY

In medieval Europe beauty was viewed with suspicion by ascetically-minded Christians as a temptation to lust and other worldly pleasures. Many later artists, philosophers, and critics have also resisted the charms of beauty, although for different reasons.

For millennia it was taken for granted that artistic creations should be beautiful, but in the 20th century many artists challenged this assumption, producing works that were deliberately ugly, or "anti-aesthetic." Given the horrors of the past century, it's easy to concede that the world sometimes demands ugly art to express its ugliness—such as Picasso's *Guernica*. One of the great poets of the 20th century, Philip Larkin, took issue with Keats, claiming that a poem could be either beautiful or true, but not both. In Larkin's grim view of existence, beauty was a lovely distraction from suffering and death, but no consolation for them.

Beauty can be a source of discrimination as well as distraction. Several research studies have shown that people who are considered beautiful tend to be awarded higher marks in exams, paid higher salaries, receive more attention from their doctors, and given lighter sentences if convicted of crimes. The pressure to be beautiful is perhaps most obvious in the photoshopped ideals of female beauty that appear on magazine covers and other media. But if we are tempted to dismiss this kind of "body fascism" as symptomatic of a superficial modern culture, we should remember the ancient Spartans, who were said to inspect every newborn child to see if it measured up to their standards of physical perfection—if it was considered "weak and deformed" the baby would be thrown into a chasm of Mount Taygetus.

Compassion

Compassion is the ability to empathize with someone else's suffering. The word comes from Latin via French, meaning "suffer with." When we have compassion we feel another's pain as if it were our own; when we act with compassion we do something to alleviate their suffering.

THE UPSIDE OF COMPASSION

It is easy to see compassion as a one-way street, where the person whose suffering is relieved benefits from another's compassion. If you recall a time someone saw you in pain and reached out to help, you will know what a powerful experience this is: even more valuable than the practical help was the fact that they *cared* about you.

But whenever you relieve someone else's suffering, have you noticed how great *you* feel? This is because compassion frees you from the prison of individuality—it takes you out of yourself, and gives you a sense of kinship and connection with someone else. By empathizing with their emotions your own sense of identity is expanded.

This is what makes the helping professions so rewarding. It is tremendously motivating to spend your days making other people's lives better and seeing the positive impact you have on them. I discovered this when I first started practicing as a psychotherapist, and I still experience it every day as a coach. No matter what problems I am facing in my own life, I look forward to every conversation with my clients, because I know it will take me out of myself and involve me deeply in their world. Afterwards, I have a fresh perspective on my own situation, and a sense of optimism that I can deal with it.

Compassion is essential for fulfilling relationships—whether with a life partner, family, friends, colleagues, or business partners.

It creates deep intimacy and trust. And when you are prepared to share someone's suffering, you can also share their joy.

THE FLIPSIDE OF COMPASSION

One problem with seeing yourself as a compassionate person is that you could end up as a doormat, unable to say "no" to others' demands, even unreasonable ones. You could be taken advantage of by people who play the victim in order to win your sympathy. If you find this a challenge, it may help to bear in mind psychologist Stephen Karpman's distinction between genuinely helping someone—even if that means using "tough love," and merely rescuing them—i.e. solving their problems for them, while relieving them of the responsibility for helping themselves.

Another pitfall for the compassionate soul is that focusing exclusively on other people's feelings and needs can become a form of Resistance. You concern yourself with others' problems in order to avoid acknowledging and acting on your own feelings. Maybe you hate conflict, so you avoid difficult conversations. Or maybe you are afraid to pursue your own dreams, so you tell yourself that would be "selfish." Go too far down this route and you end up as a self-pitying martyr, whose apparent generosity is in fact a form of manipulation; a way of making others feel indebted to you so that they return the "favor." But of course this is not true compassion.

How can you tell the difference between true and false compassion? The classic test is to ask yourself whether you would still reach out to relieve someone's suffering even if they never knew you were the one who helped them. Another way is to check in with your feelings: when you do something "compassionate," does it give you a light, expansive feeling or do you feel heavy and constricted?

Harmony

Harmony is not a sexy word. It conjures up soft focus images, in pale mauves and peach colors, of people being "nice" to each other, in a sickly, unconvincing, inauthentic way. But that is not what I mean by harmony.

True harmony is about finding a balance or blend of different elements, so that they complement each other and create something greater than the sum of their parts. We can experience harmony in the combination of different musical notes; of the tones and forms of a painting or a building; of the sound and sense of poetry; of the movements of a troupe of dancers; of the words and gestures of actors, as well as the lighting, music, and other elements of a theatrical performance. We also experience harmony (and disharmony) in our relationships with other people, and within ourselves, as we try to reconcile all the different thoughts, feelings, external pressures, and inner motivations we experience on a daily basis.

THE UPSIDE OF HARMONY

Creators of harmony work magic. Like when we walk into a room and instantly feel we are in a special place, even though each of the objects in it is unremarkable in itself; or when we are at a party, enjoying the feeling of shared happiness, without realizing how much thought, preparation, and diplomacy the host has put into bringing us all together in this way.

If they work in the arts, harmonizers are good at composition and balance; if they work in technology or business, they excel at creating complex and dynamic systems that work efficiently (and apparently miraculously); if they work with people, they are good diplomats or mediators, able to soothe ruffled feathers and reconcile apparently irreconcilable interests.

Harmony is not always sweetness and light. Dante's great poem *The Divine Comedy* asserts his vision of divine harmony and **justice**, yet the first two books, *Inferno* and *Purgatorio*, contain graphic descriptions of unspeakable torture. Within Dante's medieval Catholic imagination, however, such torments were integral to the divine order of the universe. These words are inscribed above the gateway of Dante's hell:

> Through me to the city dolorous lies the way,
> Who pass through me shall pains eternal prove,
> Through me are reached the people lost for aye.

> 'Twas Justice did my Glorious Maker move;
> I was created by the Power Divine,
> The Highest Wisdom, and the Primal Love.

(Dante, *Inferno*, Canto III, 1-6, translated by James Romans Sibbald)

Dante's poem does not simply describe this order, it *embodies* it, in the beautiful and complex structure of the verse, which is based on the number three, a highly significant number for a believer in the Holy Trinity: the poem is divided into three books which are in turn divided into 33 cantos, which are subdivided into units of three by the *terza rima* of interlocking triple rhymes. So the poem is like a fractal, with each stanza a microcosm of the structure of the whole, reflecting Dante's belief that every part of creation is enfolded within the macrocosm of divine order.

Perhaps because many of us in the modern world do not have Dante's unshakeable certainty in divine harmony, our artworks tend to be less obsessively and regularly structured. Conflict, discord, and asymmetry abound. Endings are not necessarily happy or sad; many are nuanced, ambiguous, or downright confusing. Yet precisely because of this prevailing disharmony, moments of harmony can be all the more dramatic. Like the moment in the movie *The Fisher King* where Parry (Robin Williams) spies the girl of his dreams walking through Central Station, and all at once an invisible orchestra starts playing, and the commuters are no longer rushing about but in each other's arms and waltzing in the morning sunlight.

THE FLIPSIDE OF HARMONY

Creators of harmony don't always get the credit they are due: by definition, they are looking at the big picture, and ensuring that all the different elements come together, without drawing attention to any individual elements, including themselves. So their work is often invisible: we experience the effect, but can't put our finger on the cause. I've noticed that some people who value harmony can be their own worst enemy in this respect: they focus all their attention and energy on other people and the big picture, and neglect to promote themselves and their own agenda out of fear of stepping into the public spotlight and being judged by others.

Another pitfall is that in our eagerness to avoid conflict and promote harmony, we end up glossing over points of contention, and pretending things are OK when a frank discussion, even an impassioned argument, would clear the air and create an opportunity for genuine resolution. As a family therapist I was on the receiving end of a few angry outbursts, when clients took some of their frustration out on me. It wasn't personal, it was just that I was the nearest person to hand when they were dealing with their pent-up anger. And these outbursts were often followed by a communication breakthrough of some kind. It may not have been personal, but it was anything but comfortable! Paradoxically, if you want to create harmony, you need to be prepared to experience disharmony and conflict—they are your raw materials.

Justice

The principle of **justice** has both internal and external manifestations: we each have a sense of right and wrong, fairness and unfairness, that guides our actions; and all societies have external systems for evaluating and administering justice, from the council of village elders to elaborate legal codes, law courts, police forces, and prisons.

THE UPSIDE OF JUSTICE

To most of us the value of justice is self-evident—we want to live in a just society, where people are treated fairly, wrongdoers are apprehended, and victims receive restitution.

Justice is so important that many people dedicate their lives to promoting it, as law enforcers or campaigners on social issues. Others campaign—sometimes for decades—in response to a perceived miscarriage of justice, such as a wrongful conviction or unsolved crime. When justice is seen to have been done, it brings a huge sense of relief and vindication to those affected.

If you are preoccupied with justice, you scrutinize your own and others' behavior for its ethical implications. If done with self-awareness and compassion, this can have a very positive effect. When you align your actions with your sense of justice, you experience the satisfaction of making a difference and of living in integrity. If you are brave enough to speak or act against injustice, you may suffer personally, but many societies have benefited tremendously from the courage of people who spoke up and became catalysts for change.

THE FLIPSIDE OF JUSTICE

Justice is a fine ideal, but it's hard to realize in practice. Even if you consider yourself lucky to live in a relatively enlightened society, you can probably think of numerous cases of miscarriages of justice in recent years. And you are doubtless aware of many more repressive regimes, now and throughout history, where justice is or was in short supply.

Closer to home, a fine line separates the virtuous person who acts with self-awareness from the nit-picky critic who constantly finds fault—with themselves, with others, with life in general. Judgment is like a sharp cook's knife: a useful and valuable tool, but one that requires careful handling! It also needs to be stored away safely when it is not needed. Otherwise you can spend your days listening to a nagging Inner Critic who never lets up and makes your life a misery.

Justice divides the world into good and bad, right and wrong, but in life there are many gray areas. Situations where we feel torn in conflicting directions, so that whatever choice we make seems wrong. Changes in society, scientific discoveries, and technological and medical innovations are constantly changing our sense of who we are, and raising new questions about what is ethical.

A sense that we are living in an age without ethical absolutes is reflected in the tone of much postmodern drama, which often presents us with characters who are morally ambiguous or even amoral in any conventional sense. Much of the great TV drama of recent years—such as *The Sopranos*, *The Wire*, *Mad Men*, and *Breaking Bad*—excels at making us feel empathy for deeply flawed characters. We see them selling drugs, conspiring against their colleagues, cheating on their partners, and committing brutal murders—but also laughing with their friends, kissing their children goodnight, worrying about growing bald or fat, and in moments of vulnerability with their partners. Once we've shared a drink and a joke with Tony Soprano, Avon Barksdale, Don Draper, or Walter White, it's hard to feel so judgmental toward them.

Pleasure

Pleasure needs no definition: as Louis Armstrong was supposed to have said about jazz, "If you gotta ask, you ain't never gonna know."[1] We can however identify different types of pleasure, from sensual pleasures (food, drink, sex, massage, jazz), through shared fun (parties, family time, festivals, football matches), intellectual and artistic fulfillment (creating, consuming and discussing cultural works), all the way up to what the saints and sages assure us is the ecstatic release of spiritual enlightenment.

THE UPSIDE OF PLEASURE

What's not to like? Life is here to be enjoyed, not merely endured. According to a delightful Jewish story, when we die God will meet us with a big book of judgment in his hand: he will leaf through it, sorrowfully ticking off a list of all the good things He put on Earth that we failed to enjoy. What a refreshing twist on the idea of final judgment! If you have lived a creative life, then one of the chief pleasures on God's list will be the Joy of Work.

This morning, for example, I'm standing at my desk sipping coffee, listening to Röyksopp and writing these words to you. I'm alone in the house and it's a gray day outside, but I'm having a great time; right this moment, there's nothing I'd rather be doing.

Last year I went to the Matisse Cut-Outs show at Tate Modern in London. I saw a photograph of an old man sitting in a wheelchair, playing like a child with scissors and colored paper. Entering the exhibition felt like walking into the kitchen when my kids have their paints and colored paper all over the table. As we grow older, some pleasures fall by the wayside, but Matisse's example reminds us that the joy of work can last a lifetime.

---

1 According to *The Yale Book of Quotations* the original words were spoken by "Fats" Waller: "Lady, if you got to ask, you ain't got it."

THE FLIPSIDE OF PLEASURE

If we posit a hierarchy of pleasures, with mindless fun at the bottom, writing symphonies and falling in love somewhere in the middle, and mystical bliss near the top, we can see that as we rise up, the kind of pleasure we experience becomes more intense and lasts longer—but it also becomes harder to attain.

Eating cookies and watching TV is not difficult, and it's a fine way to relax, but if you spend too long on that sofa, the pleasure (unlike your waistline) will wear a little thin. Writing a masterpiece or creating a lasting relationship is much more fulfilling, and if you do it the afterglow will last a long time—but it's also much harder to do. It's the same story with enlightenment—if you read the descriptions in the spiritual books, it sounds like an amazing experience. But to attain it, the Buddha spent 49 days sitting in meditation under the Bodhi tree, alone, in all weathers. And before that, he spent years experimenting with all kinds of spiritual practices, including nearly starving himself to death. Not many of us are willing to show that kind of commitment with no guarantee of success.

Inevitably, Resistance has a field day with the hierarchy of pleasures. *"Why put yourself through unnecessary suffering?"* it whispers when it's time to get down to work. *"Just five more minutes on Facebook, it won't make any difference. Isn't creativity supposed to be enjoyable? Why bother if you're not having fun today?"* Or it will seduce you with the pleasures of the industry "scene"—on the merry-go-round of trendy bars, private views, first-night screenings, awards ceremonies, and after-show parties.

At the shallow end, this kind of pleasure-as-distraction leads to lost time and self-recrimination; at the deep end, it becomes compulsive and addictive. At this point, the pursuit of pleasure is anything but pleasant.

Power

Power has a bad reputation—the word calls to mind evil dictators, dishonest politicians, greedy bankers, and other domineering and unscrupulous figures. When we look at the political, military, or financial spheres, it's not hard to think of abuses of power. But we should bear in mind that these are *abuses* of power, not power itself. The word "power" is related to the French verb *pouvoir* meaning "to be able to." So at its root, power simply means the capacity for action.

THE UPSIDE OF POWER

It is easier to appreciate the value of power by imagining its opposite: would you like to be *powerless*? I doubt it. Owning and exercising your personal power does not mean becoming a bully, let alone a totalitarian dictator. It means taking charge of your life, taking action, and accepting responsibility for the consequences. With power, you can make things happen for real. You can build things, inspire and lead others, and deal with obstacles, challenges, and challengers. Instead of complaining about what's wrong with the world, or the way things should be, you start to make a difference.

And believe me, you do have power. It's like a switch you flip on, deep inside you, whenever you make a big commitment—to yourself, to your goals, to whatever you truly believe is worth achieving. Maybe you have gone through long periods of your life feeling powerless, but that does not have to define your future. And when you do discover your power, it is exhilarating.

I was a late developer as a teenager, so although I loved playing rugby, I was always the smallest on the pitch. I managed to hold down a place in the school team, but it was frustrating and intimidating to step onto the field and feel like I was entering the land of the giants. A few years later at university, I played a couple of games for the college reserve team, and discovered I had caught up with my peers. I could knock people over! It felt like playing against hobbits. You go through a similar cycle of development each time you enter a new field or learn a new skill: to begin with, you lack knowledge, skills, strength, and confidence. But over time you learn and grow, and one day you find yourself speaking French, climbing sheer rock faces, managing an agency, dancing the quickstep, or flying an airplane. You have a new power.

THE FLIPSIDE OF POWER

Power is scary. If you've sat on a motorbike for the first time and turned the throttle, you'll know what I mean. You can do serious damage with power—to yourself as well as to others. And once you start to exercise your power, you are responsible for the consequences.

Power is also intoxicating. I learned this as an altar boy when I was charged with swinging the thurible to generate clouds of incense during Mass. I still remember the majestic feeling as I strode to the front of the altar, and saw all the adults sitting in the congregation waiting for *my* signal. Only when I lifted the thurible and shook it three times in their direction were they allowed to rise en masse. I don't think I did much damage with that thurible, but maybe you have had a similar taste of power and felt something of the same intoxication with it. You can probably think of more serious instances of power going to someone else's head—whether at work, within a family or your circle of friends. And that's before we consider the politicians . . . Unfortunately, it's much easier to spot the intoxication of power when it affects someone else, but not so easy to detect it in ourselves.

Many people can't handle the thought of responsibility, so they play the victim—the powerless person who is at the mercy of events and other people. The alternative is to own your power and become the creator of your future, not a victim of circumstance.

PERSONAL MOTIVATION

CHAPTER 14

Working with your values

Staying creative means staying true to your core values—here are some options for identifying your values and staying aligned with them.

- **Be yourself**
- **What are your values?**
- **What kind of situations appeal to you?**
- **Values-based decisions**
- **Warning signals**
- **Your evolving values**

Be yourself

"I want a job that doesn't exist."

I could tell Aileen Bennett was going to be fun to coach. I'd already seen some of her distinctive design work, as well as videos of her holding audiences entranced with her quirky and irreverent presentation style. Her book *Using People* was funny and full of counterintuitive wisdom. When we first met on Skype, I said she was clearly multi-talented.

"That's part of the problem. I can do lots of things, but I don't fit into any of the boxes that go with those things."

Designing logos was fun, but not challenging enough. Coaching businesses was well paid, but not creative enough. Motivational speaking was rewarding, but not in-depth enough. And so on.

"So what exactly do you do for your best clients?" I asked. And I was entranced by the answer.

She told me a story of being asked to design a logo for Todd's Car Wash in Lafayette, Louisiana. Todd wanted a new look to spruce the place up. But instead of taking a design brief and firing up her Mac, Aileen went and sat in the customer waiting area. For an hour.

"I need to sit for at least half an hour," she explained, "because then I get bored. And it's only when I'm bored that I see what customers see when they are bored and frustrated."

What Aileen notices when she gets bored can transform a business. Because, she says, it's often the little details that determine how customers *feel* about your business. The look on the receptionist's face. The smell in your hallway. The sign in your bathroom. The attitude of the staff when they are on a break. The dust bunnies in the corner. The notes behind the counter.

"The one thing I can do that you can't," she tells business owners, "is see what happens in your business when you're not there."

Once she starts to get a feel for the business, Aileen starts working her magic. She starts with the little things: adding car-themed coloring sheets and crayons in reception for the kids; baby-changing tables in the bathrooms; wifi that works; designing a thank-you card, complete with a sweet, so that customers have a nice moment of surprise as they drive away from your forecourt; creating Christmas cards from the little tree air fresheners to send out to clients.

Sometimes she coaches the owner. Sometimes she trains the staff. Sometimes she uses her drawing or design skills. Here's the sign she designed for Todd's Car Wash:

But Aileen doesn't just design logos, signs, or websites—she designs customer *experiences*.

Like Veterans' Day at the car wash. Every last Sunday of the month, US service veterans can have their cars washed for free. No strings attached. No follow up offers. Just a gift to the community. Needless to say, there's a long line every Veterans' Day, and a lot of locals who think well of Todd's business.

Aileen can work wonders, but it's hard to explain exactly what she does. No two projects look the same. So when she started coaching, her Inner Critic was having a field day.

"You can't have a job that doesn't exist. How are you going to explain it? Who are you to think you can do that?"

Aileen and I worked together for over a year, and we changed a lot of things about the way she spoke to clients and potential clients, promoted her business, and worked on her own projects. But they all started with one thing: being herself. Instead of worrying about what box she fitted into, she began celebrating the fact she is a one-off and that her work can't be described—only experienced.

CHAPTER 14   WORKING WITH YOUR VALUES

Once she did that, she had a lot of fun finding ways to help clients experience her magic and see the results in their businesses. And once that happened, they were eager for more. As a result, her income has more than quadrupled, her creativity has soared, and she gets to put her quirky little clever ideas into action every day. She's also working on a new book, and her notebook has its own popular Instagram page.[1]

I know how Aileen felt when she was listening to the Inner Critic. For years, I struggled to reconcile my urge to write poetry with my work as a business coach. I thought being a poet would put potential clients off—it would look unbusinesslike. "Most people aren't interested in poetry," I explained to my coach, Peleg Top. To which he replied: "You don't want *most people* as your clients, do you?!"

Peleg was right. I'm not a mainstream coach. And when I thought about it, clients often told me that the fact I was a poet was one of the things that attracted them to me as a coach. The more I was myself, the easier it became to find the right kind of client, and the less I needed to appeal to most people.

Maybe you're struggling with a similar feeling:

- You're good at several different creative disciplines but don't know which one to pick or how to combine them.
- You feel there's something quirky or odd about you and that some people (customers, colleagues, boss, etc.) will judge you—so at work you keep quiet about your true interests.
- You feel pulled in two or more directions that feel incompatible—e.g. business and the arts, or commercial and nonprofit work.

---

1 Aileen Bennett's notebook is online at: Instagram.com/AileensNotebook For more about her work, and her delightful Creating Clever blog, visit: CreatingClever.com For Todd's Car Wash, visit: ToddsCarWash.com

If so, take out a sheet of paper and write down the answer to the following question:

What if this thing, that I think is a problem, is actually my biggest advantage?

Write quickly, as much as comes to mind, including:

- How you would feel different
- How you would see yourself differently
- What you would do differently
- How you would talk about yourself differently to others

Over the next few days, keep looking at the sheet of paper, adding things to it, and reflecting on it. And start acting on it.

What are your values?

Clarity about your values will help you make wise decisions and follow fulfilling courses of action; a lack of clarity leads to decisions and actions you come to regret. So we will start by identifying your most important values.

If you look at the seven values we've covered so far, you will probably agree that they are all important *to some degree*—but that doesn't get you very far. So it's important to know not just what your values are, but their relative importance to each other. This is your **value system**—like the solar system in which planets orbit the sun at different distances, your value system is a cluster of values arranged in order of their relative importance to you.

1. ORDERING THE VALUES FROM THIS SECTION

Let's start with the seven values we looked at earlier. Most people tend to have a strong positive or negative reaction to these, so they will help you to get a sense of your value system.

- Adventure
- Beauty
- Compassion
- Harmony
- Justice
- Pleasure
- Power

Which of these is most important to you? Write this one near the top of a sheet of paper.

Which of these is least important to you? Write this one near the bottom of the same sheet.

Now fill in the rest of the list, until you have placed all the values in their order of importance to you.

Have a look at the list and reflect on what this value system says about you.

Now write the list out in the *opposite* order, with your least important value at the top. Imagine what kind of person would have a value system like this. They would be a very different person, living a very different life!

2. ADDING MORE VALUES TO YOUR SYSTEM

From this start on your value system, fill it out by adding more values. Here is a list of other common values that may be important to you:

- Authority
- Calmness
- Competitiveness
- Courage
- Creativity
- Decisiveness
- Discipline
- Diversity
- Efficiency
- Excellence
- Expertise
- Fun
- Generosity
- Goodness
- Health
- Integrity
- Justice
- Knowledge
- Love
- Loyalty
- Originality
- Peace
- Pragmatism
- Professionalism
- Prosperity
- Prudence
- Security
- Sensitivity
- Spontaneity
- Success
- Tolerance
- Wisdom

If you want an even longer list, visit Steve Pavlina's blog where he lists 418 values: StevePavlina.com/articles/list-of-values.htm

Choose ten values from the above list(s) and write them on a separate sheet of paper, in no particular order.

3. COMPLETING YOUR VALUE SYSTEM

Now take each of your new values in turn and place them on your system list. Maybe some of them will be even more important than one of the original seven values, so place it at the very top. Most of them will likely slot into places in between the original values on your list.

As you go through this process, you may find yourself struggling to decide which of two values is the more important. In cases like this, ask yourself whether you would rather have the characteristics of one or the other value. For example:

- Would you rather be adventurous or secure?
- Would you rather be powerful or knowledgeable?

If that feels too abstract, create specific scenarios for each value:

- Would you rather spend your money traveling the world and have amazing experiences (adventure) or buy a house and save for your retirement (security)?
- Would you rather be the head of your team (power) or the "sage" whom the rest of the team consult for advice (knowledge)?

Once you have gone through this process, you will have a list of values, in order of their importance to you. This is your **value system**. The following activities in this chapter will show you how to use this system.

What kind of situations appeal to you?

Once you are clear about your values they can help you identify the kind of work situations that will be most—and least—appealing to you. This will help you choose roles where you will have the opportunity to play to your strengths and avoid roles where you would be a square peg in a round hole.

Here's how the seven values we have looked at in this section affect your working preferences:

ADVENTURE
- **Appealing work situations:** an innovative culture, with plenty of opportunities to try new things and see what happens; minimal or encouraging supervision.
- **Unappealing work situations:** a rule-bound culture, with set procedures to follow; repetitive work; directive and controlling supervision.

BEAUTY
- **Appealing work situations:** anything involving beautiful artworks, artifacts or products; opportunities to create or curate beautiful work; attractively designed or situated workplaces.
- **Unappealing work situations:** working with functional-looking products; colleagues with poor aesthetic taste; ugly offices.

COMPASSION
- **Appealing work situations:** working with others, particularly helping them and providing a service that makes a big difference to their lives.
- **Unappealing work situations:** working alone with minimal human interaction; working for people who don't seem to care about their employees.

HARMONY

- **Appealing work situations:** collaborative teams where respect and consideration are expected; solving big picture problems involving complex systems or compositions; work with an ecological, social, or spiritual purpose.
- **Unappealing work situations:** competitive cultures where winning is a bigger priority than teamwork; fire-fighting problems and delivering short-term fixes; work that is ethically questionable.

JUSTICE

- **Appealing work situations:** meritocratic cultures with high standards; purpose-driven organizations, including nonprofits and social enterprises.
- **Unappealing work situations:** cultures where inequality, corruption, bullying, or abuse are tolerated; companies that prioritize profit over people—whether employees, customers, or others affected by their work.

PLEASURE

- **Appealing work situations:** playful cultures where fun is seen as part of the process and people socialize after work; varied, stimulating, and innovative projects.
- **Unappealing work situations:** boring, repetitive work; cultures where everyone feels pressured to work hard, work late, and look "serious" while they are at it.

POWER

- **Appealing work situations:** leadership roles; competitive environments with clear targets and opponents; healthy rivalry within a team.
- **Unappealing work situations:** "follower" roles; collaborative cultures that emphasize teamwork and deference to others' wishes.

When making a big decision about your career or business, it is wise to consider your values in this way—but watch out for the temptation to stay in your comfort zone! For example:

> "I'm adventurous, so I can't do anything boring!"
> "I'm an aesthete, so I can't do any work until my studio is beautifully decorated."
> "I'm a power player, so I need to be in charge at all times."

If you really want to live a creative and fulfilling life, you need to try new things and step outside that comfort zone from time to time. Whether you want to play to your strengths or challenge yourself will depend on your current situation and priorities. Either way, your values will help you decide what to do next.

Values-based decisions

If you are struggling with an important decision, your values can help you work out the best way forward. You can do this in two ways: by thinking it through, or by using your feelings as a guide.

THINKING IT THROUGH

1. Make a list of all the options you have in relation to you decision.

2. Take each option in turn. Look at the value system you created and ask yourself:

- Which (if any) of my most important values would be satisfied by choosing this option?

- Would choosing this option violate any of my most important values?

You are looking for the option that satisfies more of your highest values than the others, and which does not violate any of your values.

If you find that one option satisfies some of your values but violates one or more, read the section below: If you get a mixed response ...

USING YOUR FEELINGS TO GUIDE YOU

Sometimes you can spend too long in your head trying to work things out logically. When I notice a coaching client is doing this, I recommend that they switch from thinking to feeling, because feelings are often a better guide to your true values than thoughts.

1. Make a list of all the options you have in relation to your decision.

2. Start with the first option, and imagine that you have *already chosen* this option. Imagine what your life will be like from this point onwards—picture yourself making the change and experiencing the consequences. As you do this, notice the physical sensations in your body: does it feel positive (light, energized, relaxed, pleasurable)? Or negative (heavy, tense, constricted)?

3. Repeat this experiment with each option in turn. Which options produce the most powerful positive and negative reactions in your body?

You are looking for the option that gives you the most powerful positive reaction. Sometimes this is a surprise. The most obvious or sensible option from a logical viewpoint is not necessarily the one you really want!

IF YOU GET A MIXED RESPONSE...

Sometimes you get a mixed response: when thinking it through, you find that the most likely option(s) satisfy some values but violate others; or when feeling your way forward, you find yourself with conflicting feelings.

Firstly, ask yourself if this is just fear. Often, the most exciting option is also the scariest, because it means you are leaving your comfort zone and committing to a big challenge. To me, this is actually a good sign: as I said in my first book, *Resilience*, **the bigger the dream, the bigger the fear.** If this is the case, rejoice and be brave! You have found a truly inspiring path to follow.

But some mixed responses indicate a values conflict that you need to resolve before you can move forward. In this case, weigh up the pros and cons, and decide whether the conflict is a deal-breaker, or whether there is a way of adjusting the option so that it no longer violates one of your values.

Example of a deal-breaker

- **Pro:** You are offered a new job at an agency you have always admired. The work looks exciting and your first response is to jump at the chance. The job looks like a great opportunity to express your values of **creativity**, **originality**, and **challenge.**
- **Con:** The creative director—your prospective new boss—came across as arrogant during the interview process; on the way out you heard him make a cruel put-down to one of his designers and you saw the crushed look on the designer's face.
- **Decision:** The creative director clearly violates your values of **respect** and **compassion.** And you are not likely to change his personality, so you decide that this values conflict is a deal-breaker for you.

Example of adjusting the option

- **Pro:** You have been a freelancer for years, and are flattered when one of your favorite long-term clients offers you a permanent job in their studio. You love working with the team, and the role would give you a chance to do more and better work with them, satisfying your values of **excellence** and **consistency**, while adding some much-needed **security**—a value that has been sadly under-represented in your business so far!
- **Con:** You also have a product range of your own and you are concerned that a full-time gig would not leave you enough time to keep growing this side of your business. It feels as though your cherished values of **independence** and **freedom** are under threat.
- **Decision:** You negotiate a contract that commits you to four days a week at the studio, giving you **security**, while retaining one day a week to pursue your own projects.

Warning signals

Sometimes we lose our path in life and it can take a big wake up call—such as an illness, relationship breakdown, business or career disaster—before we realize we have lost touch with what truly matters to us.

Here are some of the warning signals to watch out for:

- Feeling bored, unfulfilled, or lacking motivation
- People who love you say you've "lost your spark"
- Self-sabotaging behavior and "mistakes" at work
- Getting into arguments over nothing
- Compulsive behavior—over-indulging in food, drink, sex, TV, shopping, gambling, etc.
- Feeling physically run down or burnt out

If you notice any of these warning signals, take some time out to reflect on the following questions:

- Do I honestly feel like I'm being true to myself right now and acting in alignment with my values?
- If I were unhappy with something in my life, what would it be?
- What do I really want to do that I think I can't or mustn't do?
- What do I really want to stop doing, that I think I have to do?
- What would I do with my life if I were free of the thing I hate but "have" to do?

We often get stuck when we feel we have to ignore our true feelings and values in order to meet some kind of external obligation—financial, professional, relationship, or otherwise. The answers to these questions will give you some insights into what you *want* (i.e. what is aligned with your values), as opposed to what you feel *obliged* to do (even if it conflicts with your values).

You may feel uncomfortable admitting there is a gap between the two, because that would leave you facing some big decisions and challenges. And right now, you may not know how to deal with all that. But the first step is simply to *acknowledge what you really want*. Once you do that, you may be surprised what options occur to you in the following days. When you go beyond contemplating, and make a commitment to change, you may be amazed at your capacity to find ways to make it happen, and to enlist people to help you along the way. (If you're really struggling, you may find it helpful to consult a therapist.) The good news is that if you pay attention to the warning signals, and make changes, the warnings typically go away and are replaced by renewed energy and passion for your work and life.

Your evolving values

As time goes by your values will change and your value system will evolve. Sometimes this happens in response to a crisis, other times it is simply the result of the transition to a new phase of your life. (If you doubt whether your values change, dig out your baby photos. Are you saying you had the same priorities then as you do now?)

So from time to time it's worth revisiting your value system and asking whether you need to adjust it in the light of your new circumstances. It is particularly important to do this before or after a major life change, such as:

- Starting a new job, business, or big project
- A change of career
- A promotion
- A new romantic relationship
- The end of an old relationship
- Serious illness
- Getting married
- Having children
- Moving house
- Moving country

Look at the new phase of your life and ask yourself:

- What new opportunities does it present you with?
- What new demands will it make on you?
- Which of your values will be most relevant to the new situation?
- Will there be a conflict with any of your other values?
- What values do you need to strengthen to meet the new challenges?

For example, when I became a father I discovered that several of my most cherished values—such as **freedom, independence,** and **focus**—could no longer be taken for granted. It was a real shock to my value system! But I gradually rediscovered some balance in my life by strengthening other values—such as **compassion, love, patience,** and **responsibility**—that were essential to my new role. Now, when I look back at myself before my children came along, it's almost like looking at another person.

You will go through a similar process each time you experience a major life change.

- Winning a promotion will bring you rewards and status, but also demand that you develop the values of responsibility and power.
- Moving to a new country will be an exciting adventure, but also challenge values such as security and stability.
- Meeting the love of your life is an amazing experience, but living in harmony together will also require some big changes, not all of which will be easy to welcome with open arms.

A big change is rarely comfortable, even if it is a welcome and positive one. And even the most difficult experiences can be valuable if you use them as an opportunity to learn about yourself and grow as a person. Your value system can help you navigate the change by becoming more conscious of the old values you may need to let go of and the new values you need to embrace.

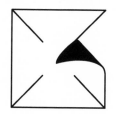

SOCIAL MOTIVATION

Influences

SOCIAL MOTIVATION

CHAPTER 15

The power of influence

Ask any schoolchild who is the greatest writer in the English language and the expected answer is "William Shakespeare." For centuries his name has been a byword for genius, his pre-eminence taken for granted. In his Preface to the First Folio of Shakespeare's plays Ben Jonson wrote, "He was not of an age, but for all time," and most ages since have agreed with him.

Yet this is not how he lived, nor how most of his contemporaries saw him. To them he was one among many—distinguished maybe, but in distinguished company. He plied his trade as a playwright and entrepreneur in a bustling city as a member of a controversial, competitive, and lucrative entertainment industry. His name was on the lips of theater-goers, but so were the names Christopher Marlowe, Ben Jonson, and John Webster, as well as others whose works are rarely read or performed these days. As companions, collaborators, and competitors, his fellow playwrights helped propel him to success.

He probably began his theatrical career as an actor before branching out as a jobbing playwright, churning out scripts for different companies. There was nothing precious about his play-writing apprenticeship, which he served in an Elizabethan theatrical version of Tin Pan Alley: plays were produced to order, for cash, on a punishing schedule, to slake audiences' thirst for new shows.

In 1594 Shakespeare took a momentous decision when he became one of the eight shareholders in a new theater company, the Lord Chamberlain's Men, later known as the King's Men when they secured the patronage of King James I. He and his partners had equal shares in the profits of the company. From that point on, he wrote and acted exclusively for his own company.

Shakespeare made a big contribution to the success of the King's Men, but so did his partners. Like James Burbage, the theater impresario who was the main instigator and director of the company until his death in 1597, and his brother Richard Burbage, the first actor to play Hamlet, Othello, King Lear, and Macbeth. Also the two famous clowns, Will Kempe who played Dogberry in *Much Ado About Nothing* and Bottom in *A Midsummer Night's Dream*; and Robert Armin, for whom the parts of Feste in *Twelfth Night* and the Fool in *King Lear* were written.

Like a modern rock band, comedy troupe, or tech startup, the partners of the King's Men achieved more together than they could ever have done as individuals. By combining their creativity and their efforts, they all increased their income. And like many bands, troupes, and startups, the money and fame led to disputes about ownership and profits. Luckily for us, a side-effect of their collaboration was some of the greatest literature the world has ever seen.

Shakespeare's story teaches us that *creativity happens between people, not just between the ears*. Whatever drives us as individuals, something exciting and unpredictable happens when talented creative people get together. They spark off each other—and sparks come from friction. From this perspective, personal motivation is less important than **social motivation**—the **influences** we have on each other.

FROM INDIVIDUALS TO SYSTEMS

In the late nineties, I was a psychotherapist working as part of a family therapy team in the UK's National Health Service. We helped clients with substance abuse problems, as well as their partners and families.

One of the unusual features of family therapy is that—subject to clients' consent—the sessions are often observed by other therapists via a two-way mirror or video camera, so that the client gets the benefit of multiple perspectives on their situation. This meant I was privileged to watch and contribute to live therapy sessions conducted by the other therapists on the team—and what I saw was a real eye-opener.

In my own practice I was used to working with individuals and thinking in terms of their personal motivations and actions. So when I started working with a couple or family, I naturally focused on the person who was abusing alcohol, or prescription or street drugs. But when I watched the family therapists' sessions, I was surprised to see that they often spent as much time talking to *other members of the family* as they did to the substance user.

When I asked the senior therapist, Ralph Gionta,[1] why he was doing this, he explained that he saw *the entire family or couple* as his client, not just the person who was labelled as having "the problem." To him, the problem was as much about communication as it was about individual addiction.

The more I watched Ralph work, the more I saw what he meant: when he helped couples or families stop fighting and start communicating better, addiction symptoms tended to diminish or even disappear. There was something magical about the way this happened, often without any need for the kind of deep inner work I was used to doing with clients. It was as if Ralph had introduced me to a Magic Eye illusion: a way of seeing a group of people not as a collection of isolated individuals, but as a group system or living organism.

---

1 Ralph Gionta now practices Family Therapy in Brussels, Belgium: 421CabinetMedical.be

Now, whenever I work with an individual coaching client, I'm still conscious of the Magic Eye illusion. As well as exploring their inner world of thoughts and feelings, I'm also aware of the many relationships that influence the course of their work and career: colleagues, rivals, bosses, clients, customers, mentors, thought leaders, and creative heroes. I help them notice and protect themselves from negative influences. And I encourage them to seek out fresh sources of positive influence.

In some cases, terminating an unhealthy working relationship or joining a group of like-minded enthusiasts, can have a bigger impact on someone's development than months of solitary effort. Yet we often underestimate the creative importance of relationships, and actively resist the idea that outside influences could affect our creativity.

WHY WE RESIST INFLUENCES

Many creatives don't like the idea of being part of a group: like the people in the famous crowd scene from *Monty Python's Life of Brian*, we like to think of ourselves as individuals. This sensitivity is usually partly the result of previous experiences, and partly also due to some popular myths about the nature of creativity and creators.

The myth of the solitary genius

These days we take it for granted that creativity is primarily an individual activity—our image of the ideal artist is a solitary genius, working away in a lonely garret or studio, or striding across the landscape lost in thought like the figure in Caspar David Friedrich's painting, *Wanderer above the Sea of Mist*. Yet this is a relatively modern image, which began in the Renaissance (when artists began to sign their works and develop personal brands), and was cherished and promoted by Romantic artists and thinkers.

The pressure to be original

Originality is another modern creative obsession. Whereas for centuries artists and their audiences were more interested in continuity with established models than in new forms for their own sake, modern artists are expected to be as original and innovative as possible. To be told you are "influenced" by another artist is not always a compliment. Some creatives are so afraid of unconscious influence and accusations of plagiarism that they even avoid exposing themselves to work by other creators in their field.

Fear of following the crowd

Early in life creators often find themselves the "odd one out" in their circle of family and acquaintances. The idea of following the crowd and choosing a conventional career path fills them with horror. But just because they don't fit in with the "usual crowd," it does not mean there are *no* crowds with whom they can feel at home. In his book *Tribes*, Seth Godin points out that we are rediscovering the concept of tribes in the 21st century, with digital communications helping us to connect with fellow creators based on shared interests.

The need to resist negative influences

Some creators have had to shut out negative voices—of unhelpful family, teachers, competitors, or other small-minded critics—in order to pursue their own path. They develop a filter to ward off evil influences, which is useful up to a point. The problem is that it also filters out positive influences.

Feeling we should do it all ourselves

Many independent-minded creatives are incredibly resourceful, motivating themselves and meeting their challenges without asking for outside help. Self-reliance is great, but there is only so much you can achieve on your own. And there is a lot of help, inspiration, and friendship out there—if you are open to receiving it.

Don't worry if you recognize one or more of these patterns in yourself—just be open to the idea that outside influences can be positive as well as negative. Especially now, when the web allows us to connect with others based on shared passions (people on your creative wavelength) instead of local geography (people who grew up in the same town as you).

THE DIFFERENCE BETWEEN REWARDS AND INFLUENCES

There are similarities between the influences we are considering in this section and the rewards we looked at earlier in this book: they are both forms of external motivation, as opposed to inner-directed intrinsic motivations and personal values. And they both involve other people, since the value of rewards such as money, awards, and fame comes from the fact that they are valued, respected, and honored by others. So they both have the same pitfall: if you depend on them too much, your creativity and self-esteem will both be at the mercy of outside influences.

Yet there are also clear differences between rewards and influences: rewards take the form of objects, whether real (dollar bills, an Oscar) or intangible (electronic money, brands, critical reputation), that represent some kind of social value. Influences, on the other hand, involve a much more direct relationship with other people, whether through face-to-face communication (one-to-one conversation, cheering or booing crowds), mediated communication (email, phone), or even imaginary communication (imagining how your actions will affect other people and their image of you).

Types of social motivation

More than most, we creatives love to think of ourselves as unique
individuals—but just like everyone else, we are subject to the influences of other people every day of our lives. Here are a few examples
of the kind of social motivations that affect our creative work.

- **Connection**
- **Copying**
- **Competition**
- **Collaboration**
- **Commitment**
- **Rebellion**
- **Contribution**
- **Tradition**

Connection

On a beautiful May morning in 2013 I was walking along Broadway,
New York. As always in this city, it was exhilarating and disorienting to walk the bustling streets where the buildings stretch up to
the sky and the sky stretches all the way down to the horizon. Yet
as I walked through the doors of the Lincoln Center and saw the
familiar 99U logo and tagline "Make Ideas Happen," I instantly
felt at home.

I had been flown over from London by 99U to coach delegates at their conference for creative professionals. That morning I met in person for the first time several colleagues whom I had worked with for years online. As the day went on, I met lots of strangers—designers, entrepreneurs, writers, consultants, coders, musicians, singers—but each time I got into conversation with someone and we shared details of our work and reasons for attending the conference, there was a flicker of recognition, a sense that we were on the same wavelength, on the same journey together.

Shakespeare doubtless had a similar feeling when he strolled through Southwark, the theater district of Elizabethan London, and saw the crowds gathering and actors preparing for the day's performances. And van Gogh as he arrived in Montmartre, the artists' quarter of *fin de siècle* Paris, and surveyed the ateliers, the galleries, and the absinthe-soaked clientele of the bars and brothels. You have probably felt the same when you first discovered a group of people who shared your creative passion, whether in a classroom or bar, at an exhibition, gig, or festival.

How can we feel so at home with people we have never met? According to Seth Godin, it is because we have found our **tribe**:

> A tribe is a group of people connected to one another, connected to a leader, and connected to an idea. For millions of years, human beings have been part of one tribe or another. A group needs only two things to be a tribe: a shared interest and a way to communicate.

| Seth Godin, *Tribes*

In the case of 99U, the **leader** is Scott Belsky, founder of the parent company Behance. The **idea** is encapsulated in the tagline:

"It's not about ideas. It's about making ideas happen."

The **shared interest** is in creating extraordinary work and a fulfilling career, and the **way to communicate** is the Conference—plus the Behance Network at Behance.net and the 99U.com magazine site. When all of these elements come together, the tribe assembles, connects, shares ideas, and starts collaborating. Each time members of the tribe connect, in person or online, new possibilities are in the air. Each individual is reminded of what is important to them, so that they leave feeling recharged and encouraged to tackle their next challenge.

I asked Scott to describe the impetus for founding Behance, and the growth of the 99U community:

> The idea behind Behance was inspired by the frustration expressed to me by so many friends in the creative world. They complained about the endless obstacles (both external and internal) that inhibited their progress. They wanted to see their ideas in the world, and struggled with the management, operations, and network to make their ideas happen.
>
> In the early days, we were just trying to solve a problem. Creative careers suffer from inefficiency, disorganization, and a lack of attribution for their work. Behance was a series of experiments to solve this problem. Of course, over the years certain efforts have thrived and the business has become more focused. Our team is now most focused on empowering creative careers via 99U, and building out the capacity to showcase and discover creative work on Behance.
>
> 99U gathers an audience of creative practitioners who deeply value their time and energy. Everyone comes with a great sense of intention. They want to accomplish something. They may be frustrated with their own progress, and/or determined to optimize how they work.
>
> Our 99U "tribe" is a segment of the creative world that sees creativity not just as an opportunity, but a responsibility. These are people who take their careers seriously and want to connect with

likeminded people and get the resources they need. Interestingly enough, we have never used the term "creativity" in any of our products and services. We see ourselves as an education and business technology company in service of the creative industry. We are not trying to boost creativity, we are trying to help people execute. I think our community really resonates with this purpose.

Just like everyone else, creators want to belong, even if it's to a tribe of outsiders, such as Bohemians, Beats, or punks. It is energizing to be around people who share your passion. You feel validated and invigorated. You find new ideas emerging from your conversation. You help each other by sharing knowledge and introductions. You encourage each other. While you're in the presence of a tribe buzzing with energy you don't have to worry about motivation.

How did I end up with so many friends and contacts on the other side of the world? It's often hard to isolate individual connections but in this instance I can trace my friendship with the 99U team to a blog post I wrote in 2007 about Action Pads for taking notes in creative meetings, produced by a company called Behance. I was intrigued by the idea of stationery specifically for creatives, so I wrote a quick review on my blog and linked to the Behance website. A few days later Scott Belsky emailed to thank me for the review, and that was the start of a conversation that eventually led to collaboration with his team—first as a columnist for the 99U.com website, and later as a contributor to two 99U books and a coach at the conference.

When I started blogging back in 2006, before it became mainstream, several people wondered aloud how I "managed to find the time" to blog. Now, I get people asking me how I came to be invited to do cool projects like the 99U books and conference. The answer to both questions is the same: one of the best things you can do to sustain your creative career in the long term is to *make time* to put yourself out there in the world and connect with others on the same path.

Copying

Shakespeare famously never invented a story. Why would he need to? There were plenty in the London bookshop owned by his friend Richard Field. He took characters, stories, and descriptions from a wide range of authors from the ancient world, including Ovid and Plutarch, the chroniclers of English history Raphael Holinshed and Edward Hall, and his own contemporaries. Here, for example, is Plutarch's description of Cleopatra, from the translation by Thomas North that Shakespeare would have known:

> Therefore, when she was sent unto by divers letters, both from Antonius himself and also from his friends, she made so light of it, and mocked Antonius so much, that she disdained to set forward otherwise, but to take her barge in the river of Cydnus; the poop whereof was of gold, the sails of purple, and the oars of silver, which kept stroke in rowing after the sound of the musick of flutes, bowboys, citherns, viols, and such other instruments as they played upon in the barge. And now for the person of herself, she was laid under a pavillion of cloth of gold of tissue, apparelled and attired like the goddess Venus, commonly drawn in picture; and hard by her, on either hand of her, pretty fair boys apparelled as painters do set forth god Cupid, with little fans in their hands, with which they fanned wind upon her. Her ladies and gentlewomen also, the fairest of them were apparelled like the Nymphs Nereides (which are the Myrmaids of the waters) and like the Graces; some steering the helm, others tending the tackle and ropes of the barge, out of the which there came a wonderful passing sweet savour of perfumes, that perfumed the wharf's side, pestered with innumerable multitudes of people. Some of them followed the

barge all along the river side; others also ran out of the city to see her coming in. So that in the end there ran such multitudes of people one after another to see her, that Antonius was left post alone in the market-place, in his imperial seat to give audience.

| Plutarch, *The Parallel Lives of the Greeks and Romans*

If that looks vaguely familiar, compare it with these famous lines from Shakespeare's *Antony and Cleopatra*:

ENOBARBUS I will tell you.
The barge she sat in, like a burnish'd throne,
Burn'd on the water. The poop was beaten gold;
Purple the sails, and so perfumed that
The winds were love-sick with them; the oars were silver,
Which to the tune of flutes kept stroke, and made
The water which they beat to follow faster,
As amorous of their strokes. For her own person,
It beggar'd all description. She did lie
In her pavilion, cloth-of-gold, of tissue,
O'erpicturing that Venus where we see
The fancy out-work nature. On each side her
Stood pretty dimpled boys, like smiling Cupids,
With divers-colour'd fans, whose wind did seem
To glow the delicate cheeks which they did cool,
And what they undid did.
AGRIPPA   O, rare for Antony!
ENOBARBUS
Her gentlewomen, like the Nereides,
So many mermaids, tended her I' th' eyes,
And made their bends adornings. At the helm
A seeming mermaid steers. The silken tackle
Swell with the touches of those flower-soft hands

That yarely frame the office. From the barge
A strange invisible perfume hits the sense
Of the adjacent wharfs. The city cast
Her people out upon her; and Antony,
Enthron'd I' th' market-place, did sit alone,
Whistling to th' air; which, but for vacancy,
Had gone to gaze on Cleopatra too,
And made a gap in nature.

These days, Shakespeare would be in the dock for plagiarism. But our preoccupation with originality is a modern development: Elizabethan playwrights worked like tailors, adjusting old creations and making new ones from the available materials. The educated members of their audience were more appreciative of works that were similar to admired classical models.

To this day, copying remains an integral part of creativity: a newcomer is entranced by the work of an established artist, and takes their first steps by imitation; they do this several times with different models, absorbing the influences and gradually developing their own style; even when they are established themselves, they will often deliberately acknowledge or draw on the influence of another artist. It's part of the game.

"But what about originality? How can we create anything new and exciting by copying the past?"

Have another look at the Plutarch, then the Shakespeare. See the difference? It's not just the difference between prose and verse. Shakespeare was not straining for originality, but he achieved it: the tone, rhythm, phrasing, and syntax of his lines are unmistakably Shakespearean. To paraphrase Oscar Wilde, he has not just borrowed from Plutarch, he has stolen, and stamped the words with his inimitable genius.

So never be afraid to learn by copying and playing with elements from other creators' work. Of course you should never copy something word-for-word or note-for-note and pass it off as your own. But each time you come across a new artist or piece of work that you love, ask yourself what you can learn, and what elements you can start experimenting with in your own work.

Competition

> "No one has ever looked at Matisse's painting more carefully than I; and no one has looked at mine more carefully than he."
> | Pablo Picasso

Necessity may be the mother of invention but sibling rivalry plays its part. Look at any period of outstanding creative achievement and you'll find rivalries at the heart of it: Shakespeare vs Marlowe; Brunelleschi vs Ghiberti; Michelangelo vs Leonardo; Voltaire vs Rousseau; Edison vs Tesla; Picasso vs Matisse; Apple vs Microsoft.

The Beatles occupy a place in popular music comparable to Shakespeare in literature, regularly held up as the pinnacle of artistic achievement in the field. But perhaps because we are closer to the 1960s than the 1590s, we are more aware of the competition from the likes of Bob Dylan, The Rolling Stones, and The Beach Boys that provided fertile soil for The Beatles' achievements. And that's before you consider the competition *within* the group, particularly the rivalry between Lennon and McCartney, as they spurred each other on to greater feats of songwriting and performance. The relationship famously turned nasty, but before that happened the creative tension between the two resulted in masterpieces that they could never have produced in isolation.

In ancient Greece, laurel wreaths were awarded to victors of poetry competitions as well as athletic games. These days, competitions are one of the most visible aspects of the poetry world—and if you think "pure" artists are motivated by nobler impulses, then you should check out Seamus Heaney's poem "An Afterwards," where he condemns ambitious poets (including himself) to the ninth circle of hell, frozen together in ice and gnawing through the backs of each other's skulls for all eternity as punishment for professional backbiting during their time on Earth.

The same spirit of competition permeates every other creative field in the countless charts, prizes, awards ceremonies, and squabbles over top billing at events. The Oscars, Emmys, and Grammys are fixtures of the calendar, as hotly anticipated and stressful as Christmas. Every year, there are commentators who deride awards ceremonies as tacky, elitist, or irrelevant to "true" measures of artistic success. And every year they are ignored in the feverish speculations, celebrations, and recriminations before, during, and after the ceremonies.

Competition clearly has a dark side, and it's not the done thing to admit you're concerned with your rivals' performance. But used wisely, competition can provide a valuable spur to your creative ambition.

Since I was at school, I've known I was a pretty good writer—I always got good grades and found myself near the top of every writing class I attended. But when I joined Mimi Khalvati's class at the Poetry School and realized that this was a room full of people working at a higher level than me, it gave me a wake-up call and inspired me to improve my own writing. Each time I submit poems to a poetry magazine or competition, I know I'm one among thousands in the editors' or judges' postbag, so I revise and polish each poem to the best of my ability before I send it off. And I'll be honest and say it makes each acceptance all the sweeter knowing that the editor plucked my poem from a pile of submissions from talented and motivated poets.

Whatever your creative field, and whatever stage you are at, you can generate a lot of motivation through healthy competition by comparing yourself with outstanding performers—your peers, those at the top of your industry, and even the illustrious dead—and challenging yourself to compete at that level.

Collaboration

As I sat in the TV studio and sipped my cocktail, I realized there's more to a chat show than meets the eye.

A few feet away Josh Zepps was sitting in an armchair and hosting *Cocktail Chatter*, the midweek news discussion show on HuffPost Live. After I had coached Josh online for several months, he invited me into the studio while I was in New York on business. I'd watched him on screen interviewing guests, including Jeremy Irons, Elizabeth Hurley, Jesse Jackson, Stephen King, and Russell Brand. But this was the first time I'd seen what happens behind the camera.

While Josh led the conversation with his guests, I could see him keeping an eye on his laptop, the autocue, and the movements of the TV cameras, while simultaneously absorbing the producer's instructions via his earpiece.

As the conversation flitted back and forth over the week's news items and related political, religious, cultural, and social issues, Josh was informed, witty, argumentative, charming, and apparently in complete control. Given that the conversation was going out live to millions of viewers, and that the sometimes controversial issues under discussion could spark a social media storm at any moment, he seemed remarkably relaxed.

It was like watching an experienced pilot keeping an eye on the mind-boggling array of instruments on his dashboard, flipping switches, nudging the gearstick, and making lighthearted conversation while navigating a thunderstorm.

As I watched him perform his high-wire act, I was filled with renewed respect for his abilities. I felt privileged to have worked with him on his career goals, including the conception and launch of his own show, the innovative topical comedy podcast *#WeThe-People LIVE*. And it was clear that although he is in the limelight as a TV presenter, he is also a team player in constant communication with his production team as well as his studio guests.

Like competition, collaboration is a dirty word in some quarters—it suggests giving up control, "design by committee," and compromise. But it all depends on the quality of your collaborators and the mindset you each bring to the work.

In the past year I have coached architects, actors, movie and theater directors, screenwriters, novelists, artists, designers, strategists, creative directors, musicians, agency owners, and tech startup founders. I can't do what they do, but by working with them as a coach, I get to collaborate with them on their creative process. To me, it's the most inspiring job in the world.

Genuinely creative partnerships and teams are founded on mutual respect and a realization that we can create something better together than we can manage on our own. Some creative industries have clearly defined roles for collaboration: advertising art director and copywriter; orchestra and conductor; a movie's producer, director, actors, and production team; and the classic rock band lineup of singer, lead/rhythm guitarists, bass player, and drummer. In other industries collaboration is more fluid and project-driven. Teams are assembled for specific productions, drawn from the leaders' network and their collaborators' networks: each new person who joins brings not only skills, but contacts and potential recommendations for others who can help.

Even free agents like me collaborate to make things happen: to create this book, I am engaging the services of an editor, David Colin Carr, to help me shape the final draft; a proofreader, Sarah Ridley, to pick up the typos we missed; a designer, Irene Hoffman, to create the cover and illustrations, and to design the print edition; and Polgarus Studio to handle the ebook formatting. Not only will the book be improved by their contributions, working with them after so many hours of solitary writing makes the whole project more enjoyable.

Give it a chance and you'll discover that, far from being a compromise, collaboration with interesting creative people is one of the best things about pursuing a creative career. Whether you're a jazz musician, an improvisational actor, a book illustrator, a theatrical lighting director, a TV comedy writer, or a college professor, you experience the same excitement at putting an idea out there to your colleagues and seeing it come back bigger, better, and bolder than it started.

Commitment

In January 2008 I was feeling frustrated and disappointed with myself. For years I had tried to establish a habit of daily meditation, without maintaining it longer than three weeks at a time. Each time I started the day with meditation, I felt different—calmer, clearer, more present—for the whole day. I *wanted* to maintain the habit. I *knew* it was beneficial to me. And yet . . . after a few days I would find myself "too busy to do it today," making a promise to myself to catch up later—and breaking the promise. Not only was this frustrating on a personal level, it was hurting my professional pride. Here was I—a coach—an agent of change—unable to establish a simple habit in my own life! It felt ridiculous.

Then one day I realized that one reason I was struggling was that I was trying to do it all on my own. I had no external encouragement or accountability. Which meant that on any given day, *no one but me would ever know* if I didn't meditate. Which made it easier to kid myself it didn't matter.

So in January 2008 I published a blog post[1] where I made the New Year's resolution to meditate every day for a year. Now

I had something at stake. Every day I was faced with a choice: keep my resolution or imagine what it would be like to admit to my readers—on my coaching blog!—that it had been too hard for me to change a simple habit in my own life.

Each time I was tempted to skip a day, I imagined how excruciating it would be to have to make excuses to my readers the following January:

"Well I tried, but you know how it is, life just gets too busy."

"Gee, who'd have thought it would be so hard?"

"Maybe next year…"

How much confidence would you have in a coach who trotted out such lame excuses? Exactly. I had now turned my professional pride to my advantage, and used it to bait a "motivational trap" for myself—just as Trollope did when he made a commitment to his manservant to get up with the coffee.

The funny thing was, the temptation to skip a day didn't arise as often, once I had made the commitment. My practice felt more real. I even found myself *looking forward* to meditating.

That year I meditated every morning apart from two days.[2] And now meditation has been part of my morning routine for nearly eight years. I can't see that changing anytime soon: it's as much a part of my routine as brushing my teeth. So what made the difference? How come I was finally able to make meditation a daily habit?

Commitment.

---

1 My blog post about my New Year's resolution: WishfulThinking.co.uk/newyear

2 So what happened on the two days I missed? Both times, I was staying at a friend's house, woke up, had breakfast in unfamiliar surroundings, and had to get going quickly to catch a train. And because none of the usual triggers were in place, I completely forgot about meditation until the following day. Oh well, nobody's perfect.

First and foremost, it was a commitment to myself. Before that New Year's Day, I realized I had not made such a commitment: I had treated meditation as a nice-to-have. Now I was committing to making it an integral part of my daily life.

Secondly, whenever you make a commitment to someone else, you have something else at stake: if you break your promise you'll lose face. This is particularly important if your commitment is linked to a part of your identity that you value highly. In my case, my credibility as a coach was on the line. For Trollope, his position as the master of the household was on the line; his authority would have been compromised if he had shown weakness in front of a servant.

Important. Commitment can help you push through Resistance and do something you really want to achieve. But make sure you start with a commitment to *yourself*, and a strong intrinsic motivation for your work. Because if your *only* motivation is a commitment to someone else—such as a contract to trade your time for money—then it's a mere obligation. Commit to your dreams.

I see the power of commitment every week, when coaching clients commit to making their dreams a reality. Like Theo Lipfert, a film director who came to me when he wanted to take his work in a new direction:

THEO LIPFERT, FILM DIRECTOR, ON THE POWER OF COMMITMENT

I had been working for a number of years making serious documentaries and experimental films. I had this nagging feeling I wanted to do something different—I wanted to write a comedy. I felt like the punk musician who wants their third album to be harpsichord only—I didn't want to undermine the work I had already made by moving in a truly new direction. Plus, I was afraid my idea might be stupid, or my writing might suck.

The coaching process was key to getting this script done. I had a Skype meeting with Mark on my calendar, and we had set a target number of pages that I needed to complete. This meant writing every day to make my quota. I would count pages as the Skype meeting got closer. Not getting pages done was not an option. I was paying for this and it was not cheap. It would be really depressing to stare at myself on Skype and hear myself make excuses. So I got the pages done.

I am not a smooth writer. It takes a while for me to get past the crappy stuff and into something good. I need to keep going, keep writing without editing, until I break out and reach something I can use. On a great day I'll write two good pages.

Commitment is a trick I play on myself to get past the garbage and to the good stuff. Commitment takes away the question, "Should I write today?" and replaces it with, "How close am I to my goal?" Commitment silences the Inner Critic because there is work to be done!

It took a long time to finish the script. But there was a psychological boost to completing the first draft. I could print it out and hold it in my hand. If I dropped it on the floor it made a noise. With a revised draft I was proud of, I started sending the script to film festivals and script contests. And today is a good day—I just got the news that *The Characters* has been awarded an honorable mention at the Williamsburg Film Festival in Brooklyn, New York (www.willifest.com/2015/screenplays).

Keeping the commitment to get the first draft written was, at the start, the hardest part of the process. But after a while drafting those pages becomes a habit you don't really think about. With the habit locked in place, the voice that screams "It's a stupid idea, you'll never finish!" gets quieter. I rarely hear it anymore.

Theo Lipfert, film director and Associate Professor at Montana State University (www.TheoLipfert.com)

Rebellion

Sometimes you need to make a racket.

These days the Impressionists are safe choices for coffee table books and coasters, but in 1863 they had to resort to an "Exhibition of Rejects" after their paintings were consistently refused by the major galleries in Paris. The exhibition was scorned by the fashionable crowd and ridiculed by the critics, but over time the public was won over and took the works to its heart.

In 1913, the first performance of Igor Stravinsky's ballet *The Rite of Spring* ended in a rumpus.[1] The "primitive" and "violent" rhythms of the music and dance shocked an audience used to a more sedate evening's entertainment. Stravinsky left the theater in tears—but Sergei Diaghilev, the ballet's impresario, said the trouble was "just what I wanted."

In 1985 the Jesus and Mary Chain played the North London Polytechnic. They stood with their backs to the audience and played a very short set, consisting mostly of loud guitars and piercing feedback. The inevitable ruckus ensued, earning them extensive coverage in the music press—to the delight of their manager, Alan McGee, who had invited the journalists to the gig.

If you've ever felt exasperated by the mediocrity and conformity of the world around you, you'll know what spurred these creators to make their mark by annoying the establishment. There's a unique form of satisfaction to be had from the expressions of shock, outrage, and horror on the faces of people who weren't expecting you or your work—and a unique form of satisfaction from finally turning the tide of opinion your way.

CHAPTER 16 TYPES OF SOCIAL MOTIVATION

---

1 The premiere is usually described as ending in a "riot," although it is not clear from the various reports whether there was actual violence, or merely a very disgruntled audience. See "Did The Rite of Spring really spark a riot?" BBC.co.uk/news/magazine-22691267

Rebels need someone to rebel against. In his provocative book *Herd*, Mark Earls suggests that social influences constitute the major unspoken motivation of human beings—and that even when we rebel against the group, we are still doing it *because of* the group.

Contribution

"I am of the opinion that my life belongs to the whole community, and as long as I live it is my privilege to do for it whatever I can."

| George Bernard Shaw

We all have personal needs and desires—we pursue the work we love, we need to be paid, and we like to be credited for our achievements, but none of these things detract from the deep satisfaction that comes from contributing to something larger than yourself—whether an art form, an industry, an academic field, or a community.

I love writing poetry, whether it is published or not. But I get a special thrill from seeing one of my poems in print. As well as the welcome ego boost, I have a sense of being plugged into the larger world of poetry, and making a contribution, however small, to the babbling conversation all poets are having with each other across the centuries.

When I was a member of the board of *Magma Poetry* magazine, which was entirely composed of volunteers, we all shared the excitement of creating something together that was of value and service to the wider poetry community—in the magazine itself, and the readings, roadshows, competitions, and other *Magma* projects. Like many creative industries, the poetry world depends on the energy of volunteers and enthusiasts, and it was a great feeling to be giving something back to an art form that has given me so much.

A large part of my motivation as a coach comes from a desire to help people—coaching clients, the people who come to my workshops or hear me speak at conferences, and readers of my books, my blog, and my free Creative Pathfinder course. Of course these things help me achieve my business goals, but they also bring me a different kind of satisfaction each time I see the difference I have made to a client's life, or I receive an email from someone who was helped by something I wrote.

If you have the kind of career or business that brings you deep, lasting satisfaction, I'll bet this is partly because you are making a contribution to something bigger than yourself. And if you are feeling dissatisfied with your work in spite of attaining some of the traditional markers of success, such as money or status, then ask yourself what kind of contribution you are making to the wider world, and what more you can give.

Tradition

Last Christmas I visited the Kabuki-za theater in Tokyo to experience *kabuki*—one of Japan's traditional forms of drama, dating back to 1603. As the curtain slid aside, it revealed a world of breathtaking beauty: a stage like a painted scroll, where actors in bright costumes and makeup acted, sang, danced, and fought. In one play, a riotous samurai battle climaxed with spectacular acrobatics. In the next, a lover driven mad by separation danced with a hallucinated vision of his former sweetheart. It was as though a book of prints by Hokusai or Hiroshige had come to life in front of me.

The actor playing the crazed lover is called Ichikawa Ebizo XI. This is his actor's title, not his birth name. Why "the eleventh"?

Because he is the eleventh member of the Ichikawa family to bear this title, most of whom have been blood relatives, with others inheriting the name via adoption. Ebizo's father was Ichikawa Ebizo X, and his grandfather Ichikawa Ebizo IX. The lineage stretches back to Ichikawa Ebizo I, who trod the boards in Tokyo, then called Edo, in the 17th century.

Ebizo I was the originator of the family's signature *aragoto* style, a form of acting in which the actor uses bold costume, makeup, and gestures to portray warriors, gods, or demons. The name Ebizo is awarded when an actor is deemed to have earned it through his mastery of aragoto. The current holder first took the stage at the age of six, and was awarded the title at 26. One day, if he makes sufficient progress, he may earn the even more prestigious title of Ichikawa Danjuro XIII—the name Ichikawa Danjuro XII having been held by his father at his death in 2013.

It is as if Shakespeare's company, the King's Men, were still performing in 21st century London, with the roles of Macbeth, King Duncan, and the Porter played by descendants of Richard Burbage, Shakespeare, and Robert Armin. Ichikawa is just one of the acting dynasties through which kabuki has been sustained over four centuries. As well as acting titles, family members inherit heraldic crests, the plays themselves, and many other traditions.

Just like the Elizabethan theater, the female roles are played by male actors, women having been banned from the kabuki stage by the Tokugawa Shogunate in 1629. Watching Ebizo dance, I was aware that his lover was played by a man, the Living National Treasure Bando Tamasaburo V; but it was only afterwards I learned to my amazement that the actor who so convincingly portrayed the beautiful young woman, so lithe and graceful in her movements, is in his sixties.

A few days after seeing Ebizo on stage, I watched a television documentary about him. The rehearsal footage, including actors as young as three or four years old practicing dance steps, made it clear how much dedication is required to reach the pinnacle of kabuki. In one scene Ebizo had tears in his eyes as he watched a film of his father playing a role that is now his own. It clearly means a great deal to him to be the inheritor of such a great tradition. His status in Japan is similar to a movie or rock star, with newspapers eager for gossip about his private life. The weight of expectation, from both kabuki tradition and the modern media, must be enormous. Yet it is also clearly empowering, giving him a deep sense of identity and purpose.

Not many arts are as tradition-bound as kabuki, but many creators feel a sense of kinship with previous generations of creators. We draw inspiration from the giants of the past, and inherit from them themes, craft skills, artistic forms, and other traditions. I was recently reading about the Earl of Surrey, a proud Tudor nobleman who was the last man executed by Henry VIII, and who is credited as the originator of blank verse and the "English" or "Shakespearean" sonnet form. I don't have much else in common with him, but whenever I use these forms in my own poetry, I can't help thinking of him and the sense of excitement and pleasure he must have felt at his discoveries.

Tradition does not exclude innovation. Even in the custom-bound world of kabuki there is scope for novelty. Ichikawa Ennosuke III is famous for extending the tradition of *keren* (stage tricks) with 20th century technology, such as his trademark flights over the audience, suspended from wires. Naturally he has attracted criticism from the more conservative quarters of the kabuki world, but he has also drawn many new fans to the theater. And keren have always been part of kabuki, which originated as popular entertainment for the common people. Like many artists, Ennosuke does not slavishly follow tradition, but engages in a creative dialogue with the past.

Cultivating your influences

Although influences, by definition, come from other people, there is plenty you can do to cultivate positive influences in your life. Here are some suggestions:

- **Find your tribe(s)**
- **Nurture your inner circle**
- **Get great feedback**
- **Use comparisons effectively**
- **Make a commitment**
- **Contribute**
- **Draw on your creative tradition**

Find your tribe(s)

This is simple in theory, even if it takes a little trial and error in practice: look for places where your tribe (i.e. the people who share your creative passions) are likely to hang out:

- In person—classes, gigs, festivals, conferences, exhibitions, bars, meetups
- Online—blogs, forums, social networks

These days the distinction between online and offline is blurred, so if you connect with a tribe in one sphere, you're likely to find ways of connecting with them in the other.

Ways to find your tribe:

- Search online—as well as using Google, use the search function on social networks, using hashtags related to your interests
- Ask friends who have similar interests
- Look at events listings in magazines, and on MeetUp.com, CraigsList.org, and other local web listings
- Visit likely venues and ask around

To begin with, you may find yourself going up blind alleys, turning up a few online ghost towns, and spending an evening or two at events where you feel a little out of place. But it will be worthwhile when you find yourself in a room or an online space full of people who are on your wavelength—you instantly feel at home.

You may well have more than one tribe. I'm plugged into several different tribes for my different interests: poets, coaches, creative professionals, bloggers, indie writers. You can have as many tribes as there are facets to your personality, as long as you have the bandwidth to keep up with them!

Nurture your inner circle

Tribes are great but they are by definition impersonal. You can't have intense relationships with everyone. So it's vital to cultivate your **inner circle**—the people you know, like, trust, and respect at a much deeper level. These are the people you turn to for support, encouragement, and challenge when you need them most. These are the people you hang out with and stay in touch with, whether or not you are currently working together. They can include:

- Friends
- Peers
- Business partners
- Occasional collaborators
- Trusted advisers such as lawyers, agents, consultants, or accountants
- Mentors, teachers, or coaches

Here are some ways you can nurture your inner circle to strengthen your support network—and theirs as well:

- Make a list of the people in your working life who you like and respect the most.
- When was the last time you spoke to each of them? Are you overdue for a catch-up conversation? Reach out and invite them to talk soon.
- Have a look at the categories I've listed above—are you missing any important roles?
- Is there anyone in your circle who could do with some help right now? If so, reach out.
- Are there people in your circle who would benefit from an introduction to each other? Why not make their day?
- Could YOU do with some help from someone in your circle? Don't be too proud to ask!
- Would it be fun and maybe productive to organize a meetup of several people in your circle?
- Is there a potential for creating a small and powerful Mastermind group with some of the people in this circle?

Get great feedback

If you want to spend your life mired in mediocrity avoid feedback at all costs. Otherwise, make it your mission to get regular, high-quality feedback you can use to make your work better. Truly great feedback is not only practically useful—it energizes you and motivates you to become the best you can be.

There are plenty of places you can get this: friends, peers, teachers, mentors, editors, or other experts. These are the qualities you should look for in a source of great feedback. Unless you are getting all or most of these from someone, move on in search of a better source.

- **They know what they are talking about**—this one sounds obvious, but it's so easy to get flustered by criticism from people who don't know what they are talking about, that it's worth keeping this firmly in mind.
- **They really care about making the work better**—it's a bonus if they like you personally, but this isn't necessarily a deal-breaker. Just make sure they aren't the snarky type who love to criticize and will do this whatever changes you make.
- **They give you clear, specific feedback**—with examples and clear criteria, not vague generalizations or blanket criticism.
- **You can do something useful with the feedback**—this has more to do with your response than what they say. If you find their words a useful springboard for action, they are worth listening to.
- **You feel energized and empowered by their feedback**—but not necessarily straight away! Sometimes feedback stings at first, and it can take a while to process it, mentally and emotionally. But if you eventually find their words a source of energy and determination, it's worth going back to them for more.

Use comparisons effectively

In the *Odyssey*, Homer tells how Odysseus had to steer his ship between the terrifying sea monsters Scylla and Charybdis. Like Odysseus, you need to confront the stellar achievements of others without succumbing to **comparisonitis** ("I'll never be as good as them!") or **professional jealousy** ("I'm better than them! Why are they getting all the attention?").

COMPARISONITIS

Comparisons are a double-edged sword: on the one hand, you can be inspired by the achievements of great performers in your field and learn a lot from their example. On the other, it's easy to demotivate yourself by judging yourself for not having (yet) hit the same heights as them.

Beware of comparing where you are *now* with people who are at the high point of their career. Use their example as a spur to improve. Once you get over the initial shock to your ego, it can be inspiring to look at others and see how much higher you can aim, as well as how much more there is to learn.

Here are some tips on using comparisons to motivate rather than demotivate yourself.

Learn from past masters

- Who are the all-time greatest performers in your field?
- Research their story and their philosophy of work and life from articles, books, documentaries, and interviews.
- What do you admire about them?
- What can you learn from their struggles, failures, and successes?
- What makes you *different* from them—in a good way?

Learn from the current champions:

- Who are the current top performers in your field?
- What can you learn from studying their work, their online communications, and what others are saying about them (in books, movies, articles, etc.)?
- Look for opportunities to learn from them in person (or as close as possible). Attend their shows, their exhibitions, their public talks, their classes.
- If you're feeling brave, you could reach out to them—but do not ask for a favor! They will be inundated with requests. Connect with them at an event or on social media—at a time and place they choose to make themselves available. Or request an interview for your podcast, blog, or another publication.
- Surround yourself with others who aspire to greatness, so that you can challenge, encourage, and support each other on the path.

Don't discourage yourself!

- Don't put your heroes on pedestals: read their stories and you'll find they were/are human too.
- Don't make negative predictions! If you find yourself saying, "I'll never achieve anything like that," change it to: "I haven't achieved anything like that yet. What can I learn from someone who did?"
- Beware of comparing yourself with your image of someone else. Don't say, "I'm nothing compared to them." Instead, focus on actions: what did they *do* that you can start doing yourself?

PROFESSIONAL JEALOUSY

Professional jealousy is a form of laziness. It's just as debilitating as comparisonitis, but the solution is simpler—accepting the reality of where you (and others) are in your career, and deciding what you are going to do about it.

Are you *really* better than the people you are disparaging? Or are you just saying that to make yourself feel better? Even if you are "just as good as them," they almost certainly made a lot of effort to get where they are now. Putting their success down to favoritism or luck is a great way to avoid the effort of building relationships and creating opportunities for your own career.

Jealousy is also a sign that you are judging yourself too harshly: at some level, you are saying: *"I need the validation of external success to feel I am OK."* So start developing some compassion for yourself, by repeating these words under your breath:

> "May I be happy and enjoy my work regardless of how successful I become."

If you find yourself resisting saying these words, you are probably still judging yourself! Keep repeating them for one minute each day, and see what the effect is after a week. Note that this little mantra does not close the door to external success—you can keep using it even if you become a millionaire superstar! But it stops you looking outside of yourself for validation.

WHEN NICE GUYS DON'T FINISH FIRST

It's harder to avoid comparisonitis and jealousy when you encounter someone who combines success with arrogance, especially if they are rude or aggressive to you.

It helps if you have the patience and the forbearing of a saint— but if not, then focus on your own interests: the more time you spend engaging with them, or thinking about them, the less focus and energy you have for your own career. Do you really want to let that asshole hold you back?

CHAPTER 17   CULTIVATING YOUR INFLUENCES

Make a commitment

If you're struggling to establish a new habit, make a big change in your life, or achieve a long-cherished goal, use commitment to push through the Resistance and finally make it happen.

1. Start with a commitment to yourself. Ask: "Why does this matter to me? What will I gain by succeeding?" Make sure it is something you passionately want to do for its own sake or for your benefit—not something you feel you "should" do to measure up to external standards.

2. Choose between making a **public commitment** or a **private commitment** to someone close to you:

Public commitments are great when you really want to put yourself on the line in a very visible way, to enlist the encouragement of your tribe and share the adventure and learnings with them.

They aren't so great if it's a very personal, emotionally sensitive issue; or if the public exposure would make you feel stressed-out; or if you don't feel ready to handle setbacks or failure in the public eye.

Private commitments are great if you have someone you can trust to support and encourage you in a constructive way, that will help you take ownership of the process.

They aren't so great if the person you choose is likely to let you off the hook easily; or to nag and criticize you if you don't perform 100 per cent successfully—because neither approach helps you take responsibility for your own success.

3. Make your commitment, including:

- A record of the commitment, such as a handwritten note, blog post, video, or Facebook post.

- Specific, measurable actions you commit to taking, preferably daily and at least weekly.
- Specific, measurable outcomes you will achieve.
- A deadline for completion.
- A channel for reporting to the other person(s)—such as regular conversations, emails, blog or Facebook updates.

4. Make it clear what you want the other person(s) to do.

Make the process clear, and make sure they are committed to it. It can be as simple as receiving your emails, liking your Facebook updates, or (for private commitments) as in-depth as a weekly meeting where the two of you review your successes and setbacks.

Do *not* ask them to chase or nag you! That's handing over the responsibility for change. You need to be in the driving seat. Instead of asking them to "Hold me accountable," tell them that *you* will be making changes and accounting for your progress *to them*.

In most cases the best thing they can do for you is to listen to your accounts, acknowledge your progress, and let you know they admire your efforts and care about your success. That might not sound like much, but once you're alone and engaged in the hardest part of your struggle, you'll be amazed how much difference it makes to know that someone, somewhere is rooting for you.

Contribute

Communities don't happen by themselves—they are created by people who show up and contribute. Become an active participant and leader in your community, and you'll find it gives you a sense of energy and purpose that you will never get by keeping yourself to yourself.

Here are some options:

- Volunteer to help at an organization or event
- Put on an event yourself
- Start a blog, magazine, or podcast that helps others in your field and makes a meaningful contribution to the conversation
- Become a helpful contributor to an online forum

Draw on your creative tradition

Every creative tradition is a treasure-trove of inspiration and knowledge. Unless you know what past masters have done—and why and how they did it—you are limiting the palette of creative options available to you. So if you are serious about your creative discipline, you need to learn about its history and traditions.

LEARNING

Run through the following list and make a note of how well you know each category within your creative field:

- Classic works
- Contemporary works
- The avant-garde
- Works from your own country
- Works from other countries
- Critical reviews and studies

Now take one of the categories you know *least* well and start adding to your knowledge by reading, looking, listening, learning and/or going to events—whatever it takes to become well-versed in that aspect of your field.

Find trusted sources of new material—libraries, websites, specialist shops. Make it easy by finding ways to funnel new content towards you. Subscribe to magazines, blogs, email newsletters.

Keep an eye out for "human filters"—critics, editors, bloggers, teachers, or knowledgeable friends—people who have their pulse on what's happening right now and can recommend the good stuff.

Do not avoid works or artists you don't like. You don't have to like everything, but if you want to be more than a keen amateur, you need some knowledge of every aspect of your field. Even if you only confirm your negative judgment, it's better to do this from an informed position than dismissing things without getting to know them. And you might even surprise yourself by finding some diamonds in the rough.

CREATING

As you deepen your knowledge of your creative tradition, you can use it as a springboard for new directions in your own work. Here are some questions that may help you do this.

- What themes from the past can I use in my own work?
- What traditional forms (genres, verse forms, song structures, etc.) can I use?
- Who are my heroes from the past? What can I create as a tribute to them, or as a form of dialogue with their work?
- What have we lost from our creative tradition? How could I revive it and reinvent it for the modern world?

Don't worry that your work will seem derivative or unoriginal. Treat these dialogues with the past as experiments, to be discarded if you don't like the results. And trust that your own talent is strong enough to mark your work indelibly as your own.

…if you are serious about your creative discipline, you need to learn about its history and traditions.

PUTTING IT
ALL TOGETHER

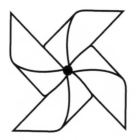

CHAPTER 18

Combining motivations

Having looked at the four fundamental types of motivation, let's return to the pinwheel and see how they combine, and how to balance them in your career.

225

1. COMBINING DIFFERENT TYPES OF MOTIVATION

We've looked at each type of motivation in isolation, but in practice you experience all four types in different combinations practically every working day. You may love your work for its own sake (intrinsic) but that doesn't mean you will be happy if you aren't paid on time (extrinsic.) You may have a strong natural curiosity or need for self-expression (personal), but you can also be spurred on to greater efforts by encouragement or competition from others (social.)

You've probably already noticed that different types of motivation can shade into one another. For example, the intrinsic motivation Purpose is closely aligned to the social motivation Contribution.

If we slow the spinning pinwheel, we can see distinctive types of motivation emerge in the spaces between the blades (see the illustration on the next page).

Personal satisfaction (personal + intrinsic)

Here we are motivated by satisfaction in the work itself, as well as the alignment of the work with our own values. This is where we

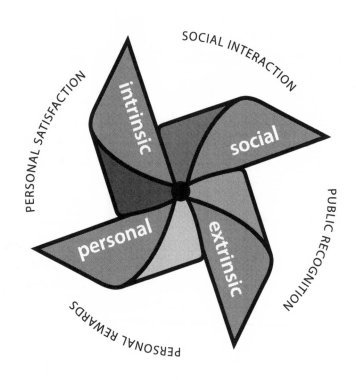

SOCIAL INTERACTION

PERSONAL SATISFACTION

intrinsic

social

personal

extrinsic

PUBLIC RECOGNITION

PERSONAL REWARDS

ALL TOGETHER

BETWEEN THE BLADES OF THE PINWHEEL

find the poet entranced with the magic of words and authentic self-expression. We also find the engineer who loves learning and adding to her store of knowledge as she grapples with a difficult challenge.

Social interaction (social + intrinsic)

Here we are influenced by each other. "Social interaction" can refer to the simple attraction of being with other people, as in "It's nice to get out of the house for a bit of social interaction." It also includes the pleasures of collaboration, and the attraction of wielding power and influence. This is where we find the mavens who love to connect others and the social entrepreneurs who want to create a business that benefits the community.

Personal rewards (personal + extrinsic)

Here we ask "What's in it for me?" We need to make sure we don't come away from a project empty-handed. This is where we have frank talks about salaries and remuneration. It's also where agents and lawyers step in to argue vigorously for individual interests.

Public recognition (social + extrinsic)

Here we are concerned about our public image and motivated to raise our profile or protect our reputation. This is the realm of awards, prizes, blockbusters, and letters after your name. It's where the critics sharpen their pencils and the crowd loads up with confetti or rotten fruit.

2. DO YOU HAVE THE RIGHT BALANCE OF MOTIVATIONS?

If you want to be miserable, focus on one motivation to the exclusion of the others. It doesn't matter which you pick: whether you're a starving artist (purely intrinsic), a sellout (purely extrinsic), a stubborn mule (purely personal), or a compulsive people pleaser (purely social), you will struggle to be happy or successful.

If you want occasional fulfillment and stop-start success, pick two motivations and ignore the others. For example, you might enjoy the work itself (intrinsic) and get paid pretty well (extrinsic), but if something in the situation means you are compromising your values (personal), you will feel conflicted; and if you neglect to build relationships (social), you will limit the opportunities available to you.

If you want a mostly-successful career or business, you need at least three motivations. A lot of the time, these three will compensate for the absence of the other one: you might be able to tolerate boring work (intrinsic) for a while if you're well-paid (extrinsic), you believe in the project (personal), and you like your co-workers (social). And exciting work (intrinsic), great colleagues (social), and a culture that lets you be yourself (personal) can go a long way to compensating for low pay (extrinsic). But sooner or later, that missing motivation will start to nag at you like a bad tooth. Stay too long in a situation like this, and you're setting yourself up for the classic mid-life crisis.

So if you want to have a genuinely fulfilling and rewarding creative career, you need all four motivations: work that is an authentic expression of your soul (personal), and so exciting you'd do it for free (intrinsic). Except you don't have to do it for free—you are handsomely rewarded for it, and you are building the kind of reputation that opens doors to more opportunities (extrinsic). You are also surrounded by interesting, charming, kind, and fun people (social). Every day brings the promise of bigger discoveries, greater rewards, new people to meet, and new worlds to explore.

Of course that promise won't be fulfilled every day. There will be plenty of struggles, plenty of setbacks, plenty of disappointments, and plenty of people eager to rain on your parade. But those are the days when you need your motivation most.

It's not easy to have it all. Which is why most people settle for less. And why there are plenty of people to tell you you're being too fussy, it's not a perfect world, or you should be grateful for what you've got. Maybe those people have a point. But if you're reading this, I'm guessing you're the type of person who *doesn't want* to settle for what most people settle for. You want to find—or better still, create—the kind of career that makes you excited to get up every morning and do great work. The kind of career you'll be happy to look back on from your deathbed.

ALL TOGETHER

CHAPTER 19

Questions to ask before starting any creative project

Problems arise when you commit to doing something based on one or two motivations, only to discover that the other types of motivation—which you'd forgotten about, ignored, or *assumed* would be part of the package—are sadly lacking.

Maybe you're excited to land a job at a top agency, only to discover the pressure brings out a nasty streak in the people around you.

Maybe you're excited to sign a contract with a major gallery or publisher, only to forget to read the small print and discover you've signed away most of the money.

Maybe you're thrilled to start work with a new client, only to discover the work isn't nearly as interesting as it looked from the outside.

I'm sure you have your own version of this experience: it happens to all of us—and to a degree it's simply part of the learning curve. But you can save yourself a lot of misery if you look gift horses in the mouth by asking a few simple but powerful questions each time you are presented with a new "opportunity"—whether it's a short-term commission, a temporary role, a permanent job, or a business partnership.

And remember that a truly successful project is one in which *everyone* involved is fired up to make it outstanding. So go through the questions more than once—firstly in relation to your own motivations, and then in relation to the motivations of the other parties involved.

If you have an open and collaborative relationship with the other people, you can have a meeting where you review the questions together. Not only will this help you avoid pitfalls, it's a great way to build trust.

INTRINSIC

What's the attraction of the work itself?

What difference will it make if I/we succeed?

Does it provide me/us with a meaningful challenge?

Does it fulfill an important purpose (beyond making a profit)?

What are the opportunities for learning?

EXTRINSIC

What's in it for me/them?

Is everyone clear about their share of the rewards?

Is everyone happy with their share?

Who will own the intellectual property created?

Who will be credited? Where? How?

Does anyone want/expect a testimonial?

Will we be entering any contests? Under whose name?

Is anyone doing this in the hope of future opportunities? How definite/explicit are these?

PERSONAL

Is the project aligned with my/our personal values?

Will anyone be working inside or outside their comfort zone?

SOCIAL

Have we worked together before? If so, how did it go?

What commitments are we making to each other?

What will happen if anyone fails to deliver on their commitment?

Will any of us be competing with each other? How?

How can we facilitate collaboration and knowledge sharing?

What kind of encouragement and support do we need to provide for each other?

What feedback loops do we need?

If I/you have concerns, what's the best way to raise them? How will we go about addressing them?

What information will be confidential? What will be made public?

ALL TOGETHER

CHAPTER 20

Five Creative Career Models

So far we've mostly looked at motivation in terms of the moment-by-moment focus of attention in the execution of creative work, as well as creative projects that last a few weeks or months. Now it's time to zoom out and look at how motivation affects the big picture of your career.

235

Five **Creative Career Models** combine the various types of motivations in different ways. Each model offers one way of resolving the tension between intrinsic and extrinsic, personal and social motivations.

1. **Lucrative Art**—getting paid to produce works of art or entertainment
2. **Commercial Creativity**—getting paid to produce creative work that solves practical problems
3. **Day Job and Night Flights**—taking a job to pay the bills and using it to fund your creative work
4. **Symbiotic Creativity**—working in two creative fields that complement each other, one of which may pay better than the other, and one of which may be closer to your heart
5. **Creative Entrepreneurship**—using your creativity to grow a thriving business

None of them is perfect: they all have their pros and cons. And none of them is set in stone: you may start your career with one model and progress through several of the others by the time you're finished. Changing from one model to another can create profound changes in your life, raising (or lowering!) your levels of creative satisfaction and income.

Changes in technology, the world economy, and society are opening up new possibilities all the time. The self-publishing revolution, for example, has created opportunities for many writers—traditionally the "poor relations" of the creative family—to switch from writing in their spare time (Model 3, Day Job and Night Flights) to making it their full-time business (Model 1, Lucrative Art). So don't dismiss any of the models because you think "it doesn't apply to me"—read through all of them, ask yourself which you find most attractive, and then start looking for ways to make it happen in your life.

1. Lucrative Art

This is the Holy Grail for many creatives: getting paid handsomely for doing the work you love. **Lucrative Art** means any creative work that is in high commercial demand *and* is valued purely for its artistic or entertainment qualities. It includes a Picasso, *Saving Private Ryan, The Sandman,* and Lady Gaga. It does not include a business website, a TV commercial, or a cookery book—these are valued mainly because they solve problems for their buyers.

Art becomes lucrative at the point of overlap between a creator's inclinations and an audience's desires. Here we find the rock stars, movie stars, and bestselling novelists, who create works that can be recorded or printed for mass consumption or performed to huge crowds. We also find the fine artists who produce one-off and limited-edition works for a few wealthy buyers who pay top dollar.

From the outside, a successful career in Lucrative Art looks glamorous and exciting—a world of mansions, limousines, and red carpets. But you don't need me to tell you how tough it is to reach this level. And even once you "make it" there are hidden pitfalls…

PROS

The most obvious attraction of this path is being paid to do the thing you love most in the world. You get up every morning and work on your art, knowing that the world is *actively encouraging* you to pursue this path.

This encouragement takes many forms—money, sales, awards, commissions, and praise. These will never be your main motivation, but if—like most Lucrative Artists—you've also experienced the opposite scenario, where the world was actively encouraging you to forget your art and do something more sensible, then you'll know what a difference it makes when the friction is gone, and you can move forward without external obstacles.

Another wonderful aspect of Lucrative Art is seeing the effect of your work on your fans—whether a stadium full of people singing along to your music, or emails telling you what an impact you've had on their lives.

Then there's the money. As you become more successful, your creativity and income form a virtuous cycle of expression and reward, propelling you to the top of your field, and bringing you a life of comfort, even luxury. The money is not just about your lifestyle: it gives you the freedom to spend your time as you please, to fund more ambitious projects, or to make a difference in the world through charitable, educational, or social enterprise projects.

Commercial success is one way of marking your professional achievement, but it's by no means the only extrinsic reward—others include awards, reviews, and exciting opportunities.

CONS

The most obvious downside of Lucrative Art is the fact it's very hard to pull off: the competition is fierce and it usually takes years of dedication and deprivation before you earn a comfortable living from your art.

But even if you beat the odds and succeed, creativity, money, and fame are a combustible mixture—and there are plenty of ways you can get the formula wrong, with disastrous consequences . . .

One of the most common is the creative who discovers that she loses pleasure in her art as soon as it starts to feel like a job: the thing she used to do for pleasure has become something she "has" to do to pay the bills. She resists doing anything as soon as it feels like an obligation, and neither the carrot (money), nor the stick (fear of what will happen if she stops), is enough to inspire her.

You can also run into trouble by becoming too fixated on external goals and rewards: as we've seen, it's impossible to do your best work if you're so focused on extrinsic motivations—such as hitting a bestseller list, or reaching financial targets—that you lose sight of your intrinsic motivation.

These temptations can be reinforced by pressure from people around you. Family and friends may find it easier to see the value of financial security than creative freedom, so they encourage you to play it safe. If you employ advisers, then even the best-intentioned will be conscious that their livelihood depends on your output, so it's always tempting for them to recommend that you do "more of what works" rather than "whatever makes your heart sing." And sadly, there are plenty of stories of creators whose success attracted unscrupulous characters who milked their clients without regard for their health and sanity, let alone their creativity.

Finally, success itself is a heady cocktail, and plenty of people have found themselves unable to handle it. Cut off from their roots, surrounded by the wrong people, hooked on alcohol, drugs, sex, or whatever—this is not a situation for the rest of us to envy. Perhaps the saddest thing of all is the fact that their apparent "success" means that sympathy and help are often in short supply: they have everything, the tabloids tell us, so they only have themselves to blame if they aren't happy.

So in spite of the glamorous image, there are plenty of pitfalls for Lucrative Artists. But that doesn't mean it's not worth pursuing, or that it can't be handled wisely.

The good news is that, as I often find with coaching clients, there is one solution that can make a difference in every single one of these areas: **return to the true sources of your inspiration, to doing the work you love for its own sake, regardless of the consequences.** It won't solve everything overnight, but it *will* put you back in touch with your superpower and remind you that you have a source of fulfillment that is always within your reach.

EXEMPLAR: CJ LYONS, NOVELIST

New York Times and *USA Today* bestselling author of 29 novels, former pediatric ER doctor CJ Lyons writes her Thrillers with Heart for the same reason she became a doctor: because she believes we all have the power to change our world. In the ER she witnessed many acts of courage by her patients and their families, learning that heroes truly are born every day. Two-time winner of the International Thriller Writers' coveted Thriller Award, CJ has been called a "master within the genre" (*Pittsburgh Magazine*) and her work has been praised as "breathtakingly fast-paced" and "riveting" (*Publishers Weekly*). Learn more about CJ's Thrillers with Heart at CJLyons.net

What made you want to be a writer? What aspects of writing do you enjoy the most?

I've been a storyteller all my life—it got me into a lot of trouble when I was a little kid! Telling stories has always been my way of coping with the chaos surrounding me, making sense of the "real" world.

I wrote my first novel when I was fifteen and two science fiction novels in med school, but never seriously thought of publishing as a career until years later when fellow members of a writing group convinced me to enter a national writing contest. I was a finalist, which garnered me the attention of agents and editors, and eventually my first contract.

After my second contract, I realized I couldn't give both my patients and my writing 120 per cent of my time and energy, so I took a leap of faith and left my pediatric practice to write full time. It was terrifying, but well worth it—I've been supporting myself with my writing for over nine years now.

I honestly can't not write—it's an addiction and I get withdrawal symptoms (itchy, crawly feeling under my skin, agitation, talking to myself, irritable) when I try to take a few days off.

It's really difficult to decide on one favorite aspect! There's that wonderful anything-is-possible feeling when you're just starting a story, playing with characters and themes and all those tantalizing "wow, what if?" questions. But when you're in the heart of a story and waking every morning with the characters talking in your head and the words just flow, there's an indescribable joy in that, truly a sense of "following your bliss."

Then, after a book is done and in the hands of readers, there's this nervous, tingly feeling of stage fright on opening night. But as soon as that first fan letter comes in, thanking you for changing someone's life with your words and imaginary world, it's quickly replaced with a euphoria that can't be beat.

Do you think of your ideal reader during the writing of a story? If so, does this differ from the way you think of your readers when it comes to marketing your books?

During the writing process, my first drafts are for me, me, me … I'm really selfish as I explore a new story and different options, without caring if they are commercially viable.

As soon as I have a story finished I switch modes and divorce my ego from the process, putting my readers first as I make editorial decisions. Every slice and dice, each plot twist, each scene is now focused on my mantra: will this delight and excite my readers?

Often this is the most difficult part of the process. Telling the story the first time when it's only for me is fun … deciding what stays and what goes and what gets tweaked is hard, hard work. I'm always terrified when I release a new book (yes, even after 29 books, I still get that queasy feeling on release day!) that I've somehow let my readers down . . . but then the fan mail and reviews start pouring in and I'm reassured . . . until the next book!

Once the book is done and it's time to make business decisions, I keep my readers front and center with the same mantra: will this delight and excite my readers?

So instead of spending a week at a writers' conference and not getting any writing done, I'll stay home and write because my readers want more books published faster. BUT if that's a week at a readers' convention where I can meet and greet my fans, then I'll do whatever it takes to see those fans and connect with them.

How and when do you think about external goals, such as numbers of books sold, bestseller charts, money, and reputation?

I'm one of those people who is very internally driven—if I want to do something, no matter the cost or effort (such as a girl like me from a small town in Pennsylvania leaving at 17 to go to college and then working three jobs to put herself through medical school), if I think it's right for me, I'll figure out a way to do it. It might take years (like deciding to pursue writing as a second dream-come-true career), but I'll get there.

So that's all about turning a dream (something out of my control) into a viable goal that I can work toward and achieve.

But those externals, things that really aren't in your control like bestseller lists, or how many people decide to buy your books, and what they think about them? Those really don't factor into my day-to-day thinking because they aren't part of my definition of success.

Yes, there are ways to put a book on bestseller lists and yes, you can convince tons of people to buy your books—but those are tactics, not the end goal. How people feel about a given book, that's also beyond my control. Sometimes I pour my heart and soul into a book and not all my readers are as delighted and excited as I hoped.

Writing and selling stories may be how I pay the bills, but it's not WHY I write. Simon Sinek has a wonderful book called *Start with Why* that crystallized this crazy storytelling thing I've been doing all my life. When people ask why I write, the answer is to make sense of the chaos in this world . . . and to find the courage to change it. (That's also why I became a pediatric ER doc.)

This is why every story I tell features everyday heroes, ordinary people who have found the courage to make a stand. The heart of my stories isn't in the thrill of a world-changing climax (James Bond defusing the nuclear warhead) but rather in the quiet, heartfelt struggle it takes to find the courage to try to save a character's world: family, friends, home.

By creating my own sub-genre of "Thrillers with Heart," I set my goal of writing stories filled with emotional honesty, and I attract readers who resonate with my kind of stories.

Which gives me a clear path to success (as I measure it): write the stories that fulfill the promise of a CJ Lyons' Thriller with Heart, delighting and exciting them so much that they pay me for the privilege of sharing their time and attention with me while telling their friends about my books.

If I keep my readers happy by delivering on my promise to them, they keep my bottom line happy.

Your *Buy a Book, Make a Difference* project is clearly very close to your heart—can you explain what it is, and what motivates you to do it?f

When I was young, I wrote science fiction and fantasy. I didn't turn to writing crime fiction and thrillers until my internship in Pittsburgh when one of my fellow interns was murdered.

It was a horrific crime, thankfully solved due to the hard work and cooperation of three Crime Scene Units (city, county, and state). After I was published, I dedicated several novels to Jeff's memory, and once I started hitting the bestseller lists and making pretty good money, I established the *Buy a Book, Make a Difference* charity foundation.

Together my readers and I raise money for worthy charities and also provide scholarships for underserved community police officers to get forensic training they couldn't otherwise afford. So far we've raised almost $80,000 and have given away 72 forensic scholarships—so there are now 72 less places in this country where you can get away with murder!

If anyone knows of a police department that might need a little extra help, they can learn more at CJLyons.net/heroes

2. Commercial Creativity

Commercial Creativity is creative work that is in high demand *and* is valued mainly for its usefulness, not purely as art or entertainment. It includes activities as diverse as website design, marketing campaigns, nonfiction books, educational programs, new product design, and instructional videos. All of these can of course be produced to high aesthetic standards, and can give pleasure in their own right. But the *primary* reason their customers buy them is to solve a problem—to attract customers of their own, learn skills, create products, and so on.

Practitioners of Commercial Creativity include copywriters, art directors, designers, editors, teachers, nonfiction authors, programmers, coaches, and consultants—all of whom place their creativity at their customers' service, helping them solve problems and reach goals.

Some people see the very idea of Commercial Creativity as a contradiction and compromise, holding their hands up in horror at the idea. But others find this a path that is very rewarding creatively, financially, and personally.

PROS

As the name suggests, Commercial Creativity can be the path to riches, bringing you a nice lifestyle and the freedom to spend time on whatever side projects—artistic, charitable, or otherwise—take your fancy. But having coached plenty of Commercial Creatives, one thing I've noticed about the happiest and most successful of them is that money is just one of several motivations that drive them.

As with Lucrative Art, one of the biggest attractions of Commercial Creativity is the prospect of getting up in the morning and knowing you will be doing the creative work you love all day—and getting paid for it. The happiest Commercial Creators are the ones who find clients and commissions that inspire them, so that they are thrilled to work on each new project, and proud to point to their work afterwards.

They don't see a conflict between creativity and usefulness: if they are service providers, they *enjoy* the challenge of solving a client's business problem through their creativity. If they are creating useful products, they love the fact they are helping their customers. In other words, they have strong intrinsic motivation for the big-picture task, not just the creative execution via writing, design, filming, or whatever.

The best service providers also have the confidence to select their clients carefully, only taking on their ideal clients: the ones who inspire them (intrinsic motivation), who are fun to work with (social motivation), and whose businesses they believe in (intrinsic motivation: purpose).

CONS

One of the most obvious drawbacks of Commercial Creativity is the "nightmare client/boss/company": we all know creatives who complain about the people at work whose unreasonable demands make their working lives a misery. This is no joke, but it's actually not specific to the Commercial Creativity path: look around you, and you will discover there are toxic people in all walks of life—part of the game of life is spotting and avoiding them.

Fortunately the solution is simple; unfortunately it is rarely quick and easy: **find better people to work with**. If you're self-employed, fire your clients and find better ones. If you're an employee, start looking for another job.

One of the biggest pitfalls of the Commercial Creativity path is choosing it as second best to Lucrative Art—which seems unattainable. In this scenario, working in a commercial environment feels like a compromise from the start, so a part of you resents the constraints of a commercial environment. This is understandable:

rock stars and bestselling novelists don't achieve fame and fortune overnight, and there are bills to pay in the meantime. So in the short term it makes sense to use your talents in a Commercial Creative field. But compromise is not a long-term solution. If you want to avoid frustration, disillusionment, and potential burnout, you have two basic options.

One way forward is to find strong intrinsic motivations for the Commercial Creative work you do. Look at the big picture of your work and its potential impact—on clients, customers, an industry, or society. Ask yourself: *"Is there anything here that inspires me? Is there an opportunity to make an important difference?"* You may discover something you'd overlooked before, or you may need to make some adjustments to your situation.

For example, if you're a freelance copywriter bored with writing website copy for small businesses, you may need to learn more about your clients in order to discover something really interesting—for you, for the business itself, and for their customers. Or you could decide to focus on a type of business that genuinely excites you, to get more interesting commissions and become the go-to expert in your field. If you're a snowboarder, write for snowboard manufacturers; if you love horses, write for stables; if you're a martial artist, write for companies in that space.

The second way forward is to decide that Commercial Creativity is just a stepping stone for you—a way to pay the bills and hone your skills while you pursue a side project that will eventually become your main gig. Which we'll explore in our third Creative Career Model…

The happiest Commercial Creators are the ones who find clients and commissions that inspire them...

EXEMPLAR: JOHAN ADDA, USER EXPERIENCE DESIGNER

Johan Adda is a seasoned user experience designer who has worked on mobile products you have probably used many times. Before he could write, his mum—a designer for Hermès—used one of his drawings as the inspiration for an Hermès scarf. He went on to become an entrepreneur, in-demand designer, speaker, and now a teacher. He is on a mission to save the world from bad design by teaching UX design via free and paid courses at: MissionUX.io

What exactly is User Experience Design and what made you choose to work in this field?

There are lots of ways to define UX Design. It took me +10 years to find my own definition: "A good user experience respects, helps, and delights anyone who encounters your product or service."

To illustrate this definition, let me tell you a story. It's about "cho-co-lat." (You may notice my French accent—we pronounce every syllable.) Go take a piece of dark chocolate and pop it into your mouth. Do not bite it—keep it melting in your mouth until the end of the next paragraph.

If the chocolate maker has done his job well, 600 exotic molecules will be released in your mouth and nose. As it becomes more liquid you experience fruity and nutty flavors, followed by a cooler sensation on the tongue. It's even better if you close your eyes and feel the warm chocolate melting in your mouth.

That's my job. I am not a chocolate maker of course. But I love mixing technology (such as melting dark chocolate chemical reactions) with users' needs and desires, and shaping the concoction into experiences. Most of my time is dedicated to understanding where people are struggling using a phone, a PC, or a web service, and making it easier for them to get what they want from it.

I'm really glad I made the decision years ago to enter this field. Since then I have influenced million of lives, and that's quite an amazing sensation. To respect, help, and delight people is a good reason to get up in the morning.

Why does User Experience matter?

There is a beautiful story about a children's hospital in New York which has designed its brain scanning room with a pirate theme. They painted a bold and colorful decor all around the scanner itself, and put some pirates on the walls. The bed looks like a boat. That's a lovely example of changing a scary process into a more welcome experience.

A few years ago I was working at Orange, the French telecom. One day a manager came to our UX team with bad news. He was holding a printed email from a customer telling him that he just received a €7,500 bill (about £5,280 or $8,200). This father had given his old iPhone to his teenage son to travel to New York. What the kid did was usual behavior—surfing the net, Instagramming his photos, etc. That was OK at home, but definitely not abroad! Orange refunded the customer, and our team was charged with alerting people when they reached a cap. If no action was taken, we decided to stop the data leak after the second alert. I like to think we helped a lot of customers save money.

Another time I helped a charity increase the effectiveness of their website. I made the "donate" button 30 per cent bigger and heightened the colors to make it stand out. They increased their donations by 20 per cent. It took me 3 minutes to do that—and 15 years of experience.

When and how do you think about external factors, such as money, awards, professional reputation, and public recognition?

Let me start with the last one, public recognition. It is not a priority—but it is sweet to be interviewed here, let's be honest!

The best compliment I received in my entire working life was during a user test. We asked a user if he had anything to say about the interface—the "skin" of the service he was testing. His answer still resonates for me: "Which interface? I don't see any interface!" Wow. We nailed it! This guy was so immersed in the content that he barely noticed the interface. That's my goal. If users notice my work it means we need to redesign it.

Money is an important factor in our field, but this is quite a recent development. It used to be that tech was a hobby for enthusiasts. Now it is woven into the fabric of our lives. So our challenge today is making something—such as an app, a start-up, a service—that generates a lot of traction, and that requires a deep understanding of customers' needs, desires, and behaviors. If you do it well, you can sell it to big tech companies and make a lot of money. So we have come a long way!

Professional reputation is not really a concern. I enjoy listening and reading opinions from my peers, but my voice and my ideas are for the customers first.

Who are the most important people in your working life, and how do their influences affect you?

I carefully listen to my favorite non-geeky, adorable, best user—the mother of our son, my girlfriend. She reminds me that most people are not interested in User Experience!

Every day, discreetly, I watch a lot of people using their phone—the way they hold it and interact with it. Human behaviors are my dope, if I'm honest.

I also find mentors outside my field. For example, at the moment I am studying cartoon animation from Disney's gurus. One book, *The Illusion of Life*, is about reproducing some human movements, gestures, and expressions with a touch of exaggeration to make cartoons more funny and realistic. It's giving me hints and ideas I can use in my own designs.

I have one special mentor, and I would love to time travel and meet him. He was an actor, an engineer, a painter, sculptor, poet, a war counselor, an amazing party organizer—and I'm probably missing some of his roles. We all know him: Leonardo da Vinci. He was good at keeping his brain active, always. I tried one of his tips: if you can do one thing with your right hand, try to do another thing with the other. Try it, it's fun.

Right now, I'm helping other designers to respect, help, and delight their users and customers. My blog, Mission UX, is all about that—if you're a designer who wants to become a user experience generalist, I offer free training, and I'm working on some paid courses. Who knows, one day it could become a book too. It's my way of making a contribution to my field—and helping to create a better-designed world for all of us!

The last influence is my son. I find it quite cool to imagine telling him one day in the future that I have written a book about "chocolat" and user experiences...

Au revoir.

3. Day Job and Night Flights

Day Job and Night Flights means taking a job that you either enjoy or can at least tolerate with good humor, which gives you financial security, peace of mind, and a reasonable amount of spare time. You then use this time for your own creative projects.

For many, this is a temporary stage, almost a rite of passage: the actress waiting tables while she pursues her big break; the novelist scribbling away at weekends on the masterpiece that he hopes will bring him fame and fortune; the aspiring entrepreneur using her paycheck and evenings to start the business that will help her escape the cubicle.

For others, the day job is here to stay. Many creators prefer things this way. When asked why he worked as a librarian, Philip Larkin replied that it was only possible to write poetry for two hours a day, and the job kept him out of trouble. Wallace Stevens enjoyed a successful career as an insurance company executive while writing his whimsical and enigmatic poetry.

In this model, the day job is not necessarily uncreative—lots of people work 9–5 in commercial creative fields and pursue their artistic interests in the evenings and weekends. The difference between this model and the next one—Symbiotic Creativity—is that for Symbiotic Creatives, there is an important link between their different creative disciplines; whereas the Day Job and Night Flights are pursued independently, even if both are creative.

PROS
Probably the biggest creative benefit of the Day Job and Night Flights path is the fact your art never has to earn its keep: you're completely free of financial considerations, so you can do what the hell you like. There's no temptation to compromise or sell out. And since it never becomes a job (a pitfall of Lucrative Art) it feels like an escape from the daily grind.

Financial security doesn't sound very Bohemian, but if you've ever been stressed about next month's rent, you'll know *that* isn't a very creative state of mind. When you don't have to worry about money, it frees up your mental bandwidth for more exciting thoughts.

A decent paycheck also means you can afford the books, shows, and experiences that feed your imagination, plus high-quality equipment and supplies to work with. I know several musicians whose day jobs have paid for very well-equipped home recording studios, as well as photographers with high-end Macs and state-of-the-art printers.

Even if there's never any money in your Night Flights, there are other extrinsic rewards that bring a different kind of satisfaction: Wallace Stevens received widespread praise from critics and his fellow poets, and won a Pulitzer Prize for his *Collected Poems*.

CONS

Day jobs can be all-consuming—if you're not careful, yours could consume your creativity. In the worst-case scenario, your job is a soul-destroying grind, and it's hard to create something amazing if it feels like your soul is under threat. If this is the case, you need a new job—or a new Creative Career Model.

Even if you basically enjoy your work, it can take up so much of your time and energy that there's very little left over for creating. This is particularly true for information workers: if you spend all day staring at a screen, it can be hard to muster enthusiasm for staring at another computer screen all evening. Whatever your line of work, it's important to remind yourself that your creativity is something you *want* and *choose* to do. If it ever starts to feel like another obligation, then challenge yourself to give it up—if you try this, you'll likely soon remember why you loved it in the first place.

It can be frustrating if you feel that your art is relegated to the status of a hobby, and if you wish you had more time to realize your potential. In spite of his remarks about needing to fill his day, Larkin also said in another interview that most of his poems had been written in the evenings after a long day at work; he wondered whether they might have been better if he had been free to work on them earlier in the day.

Another pitfall is **Superman syndrome**: by night you're a creative super hero, possessed of magical powers—and maybe an audience which sees you as a minor celebrity. Yet every morning you have to clock into work with people who neither know nor care about your other identity. To them you may be an unremarkable Clark Kent-type. You don't need to be an egomaniac of the "Do you know who I am?" variety to find this a little disorientating or galling. On the other hand, I know a few creatives who love having the ability to both blend into the crowd during the daytime, and then escape into their alter-ego at night…

EXEMPLAR: SCOTT PURNELL, SONGWRITER AND GUITARIST, SECRET SHINE / CREATIVE DIRECTOR, REAL DESIGN AND MEDIA

Scott is a 44-year-old musician, graphic designer, enthusiastic amateur athlete, and father of two beautiful daughters. In 1990 Scott and Jamie Gingell founded the band Secret Shine (Facebook.com/SecretShine) with a handful of song ideas and a Foster X26 4-track recorder. Their first demo landed them a deal with legendary Bristol label Sarah Records. Scott, Jamie, Dean Purnell (Scott's brother), and Kathryn Smith have been the mainstay of the band for 23 years, releasing three albums and a string of EPs and singles, with a fourth album due in 2016 (SecretShine.BandCamp.com).

In 1999 Scott and Cathy McKinnon started a design studio, Real Design and Media (RealDesignandMedia.com). They wanted to pursue their own creative paths (Cathy, acting and Scott, music) as well as designing by day—the flexibility of working for themselves made this possible. In 2003 Dean joined the business and the three of them remain the directors of Real Design and Media.

How did you end up with two such different roles? How do you divide your time between your band and your design studio?

Ever since I heard my first pop records in my pre-teens I knew I wanted to play in a band. I started writing and performing in Secret Shine when I was 19, having already been in the indie-dream-pop band Dreamscape for two years. My songwriting partner in both Dreamscape and Secret Shine, Jamie Gingell, got a place at Bournemouth University midway through the recording of the demos for our first EP/album on Sarah Records—so I piggy-backed him onto the same course to keep our creative dream alive. 25 years later we're still together, still writing songs, but not quite as prolific as we used to be!

I graduated from Bournemouth Uni in 1993 with a degree in "Communication and something not relevant to any job"—but luckily an open-minded interviewer at Future Publishing in Bath thought I had the potential to make it in graphic design. I loved being a designer from my very first day at Future. It was a time when magazine sales were booming and healthy profits allowed you to be creative, without the tight deadlines and budgets we have now. I spent six years at Future, progressing to Deputy Art Editor of *Guitarist* magazine before I left to start my own company.

Dividing the time between music and paid work is pretty simple. By day I'm a designer and a business owner—that is my priority or the mortgage doesn't get paid, so rehearsals and songwriting sessions are almost always in the evening or at weekends. Secret Shine are not prolific performers, but in the last eight years we have played three small tours of the States, as well as traveling to play in Germany, Sweden, Denmark, and Spain. We also recorded our new album, for Saint Marie Records (SaintMarieRecords.com), in the south of France last year, when the whole band decamped to a studio in the Pyrenees. This does impact on our paid working hours, but all the band members are lucky to have lots of flexibility in our jobs.

What do you love about making music? How different is this to your motivation for your design work?

I love the joy of picking up a guitar or tinkering away on a keyboard and from a random idea something growing, evolving, going on its little journey to becoming a song that's recorded or performed. I remember one sunny afternoon cutting my lawn and hearing a melody in my head and then running inside to play it on my guitar and record it into my phone before I forgot. Six months later I was playing that song with the band to a few hundred people at a festival in Denmark. Not every song makes it past infancy of course, but when they do it's very magical and incredibly soul-enriching.

When I started to read this question I thought my motivations for design and music might be polar opposites, but in the course of answering I realize they are very similar.

In my day job I have to be able to bring money into the business to cover our overheads; however my motivation is not singularly financial reward but to be creatively satisfied with the work I produce. A satisfied customer brings in money and repeat business, but this is more a necessity than a primary motivation.

There are many contrasting motivations with being in a band such as the experiences of recording, playing, and traveling together, signing records or hearing feedback from fans, watching people dance or sway to your songs at gigs. However, creatively I take an equal amount of pride in any piece of work I produce, whether it's design or music. The principal difference is that as a band, we don't have to stick rigidly to a brief, and are not bound by commercial pressures or deadlines from the record label or an audience.

Some people experience a greater sense of creative freedom when there is no pressure on them to earn a full time living from their artistic work. Do you find this?

I can find creative freedom in both design and music. Even when a design fee is involved, if you have worked with a client for years, and they understand and like your style, they will allow you room to maneuver and express yourself. These opportunities are more limited in the design environment than in music, where there are very few commercial pressures, but it is possible to find a creative and financial balance.

**Are there any downsides to having limited time for
your music?**

Making records becomes a very long drawn-out process. For
instance, we started demoing our latest record in 2012. Having laid down basic tracks for about 18 songs we finally got
the band to decide on ten to record together in a studio in
France in September 2014. It took about nine months to find
a date when all five band members and the sound engineer
could travel to France together. A year later we are only just
starting to mix the record! I expect the record to come out in
2016—five years after our last one. The major downside is that
the songs are about four years old by the time they come out.
It's the same with playing gigs—it's very rare the band are all
available on the days we are offered gigs. This year we had to
turn down an appearance at New York Popfest!

**Is it ever disorienting to have two different identities?
What is it like to come off stage to rapturous applause from
your audience then go to work the next morning?**

It is strange at times. In 2013 we played three dates at the
Culture Collide festival in Los Angeles, and were treated like
musical royalty by the festival organizers and Tuti, our chap-
erone. On the last day we played a buzzing gig in LA, signed
records, met old (and new) fans, and then were driven to a Pet
Shop Boys gig. Following that gig we were chauffeured to Vegas
and entertained in the Bellagio at 4 a.m.

    The next day Tom the drummer and I got on a plane back
to LA, then on to Heathrow, then a coach back to Bristol—and
by late afternoon I was sat in my office working on magazine
pages. That was pretty surreal!

Who are the most important people in your creative life? How are you affected by their influences?

In my early life my parents were a significant influence. I remember their love of pop music and Sunday music nights, where I would drift off to sleep with the sound of The Carpenters, Queen, or The Beatles coming from downstairs. My mum put my brother and me into piano lessons from quite an early age and I would always play along to songs on the radio. They were also creative in different ways—not great painters or writers, but we would win every fancy dress competition. They took great care and detail to create amazing home-made costumes. My dad is a builder and again, I admire his attention to detail and imaginative problem solving.

More overtly I was very influenced by my business partner Cathy—when I joined Future, I recognized straight away she was where I wanted to be as a designer. She has a particular quality, style, and confidence in her work that you can't learn, but just try your best to live up to. Again it's an attention to detail, creative imagination, and doing every piece of work to the same standard, whether it's a simple layout job or styling a fashion photo shoot.

So many musical influences in terms of bands and songwriters, but again the direct influence comes from my piano and guitar teachers, who didn't just teach the technicalities of playing an instrument but the passion required to be more than just a player. My guitar teacher in particular would let me stay on after lessons and listen through all her amazing records. My fellow songwriter Jamie has been my biggest inspiration—his ear for melody is second-to-none, and I feel he should write many more songs for other artists. Our creative competitiveness, cooperation, and compatibility has possibly been my biggest motivation during my 25 years in music.

4. Symbiotic Creativity

In the **Symbiotic Creativity** model you pursue two (or more) creative fields simultaneously: one is your primary artistic calling, which may or may not earn you much money; the other is in a related creative field which offers a more stable income.

In biology, "symbiosis" means different species living together for mutual benefit, such as the pilot fish that swim unharmed with sharks and eat the parasites from the sharks' skin; or the clownfish that has developed immunity to the sea anenome's stinging tentacles, benefiting from their protection while eating small invertebrates that prey on the anenome.

In this model we find the artists, writers, actors, musicians, and film-makers who are university professors, teaching their art to students; the guitarist who gives guitar lessons; the artist who creates installations or delivers training for corporations; and (ahem) the poet who helps his fellow creatives with books and coaching.

This path is similar to Day Job and Night Flights, but here there is no rigid separation between their daytime work and the creative projects they pursue in their spare time: Symbiotic Creators say their disciplines are so intertwined they would find it hard to do one without the other.

As the name suggests, the Symbiotic Creative disciplines are mutually supportive: whether or not you earn much money from your work as a choreographer, it can help you land a lecturing job, and will inform the content and style of your teaching; similarly, writing and lecturing about choreography will prompt you to reflect on your artistic practice and may well influence it.

Personally, my life would be unthinkable without poetry. I earn my living as a coach, but my coaching would likewise be unthinkable without the poetry: it developed out of my fascination with the creative process. And let's face it, I wouldn't have much credibility as a coach encouraging others to pursue their artistic dreams if I weren't pursuing my own.

PROS

If you get the balance right, Symbiotic Creativity can feel like the best of all possible worlds: you don't have to divide yourself into "creative" and "professional" selves (as with some Day Jobs and Night Flights) and you get to spend all your time working in creative fields. You are free to pursue your art without compromise or the temptation to sell out (as with Lucrative Art), knowing that you have a reliable income.

Many Symbiotic Creators say that a change is as good as a rest. When you get tired or stuck in one field, you can switch to the other with a sense of relief. I love having poetry as a space I can enter where none of the usual rules apply. Conversely, after hours of sitting on my own with a notebook, I look forward to my next coaching client and the opportunity to immerse myself in *their* world.

CONS

Have another look at the Pros of Symbiotic Creativity, and note the "if" in the phrase "if you get the balance right…" As with the other models, there are several ways you can get the balance wrong.

If one of your disciplines earns you more money (or brings you more fame and reputation) than the other, then you can feel a subtle (or not-so-subtle) pressure to spend more time on it. The time you devote to your art can feel like it's costing you money, so you feel the need to justify it, even if only to yourself.

If you give in to this pressure and neglect your art, it will slow your progress and lower your confidence. You can start to feel like a fraud: *"Who am I to teach / talk about this stuff when I'm not doing it myself?"*

Or you might have the opposite problem: you enjoy your artistic work so much, and it's *sort of related* to the work that pays the bills, so you find yourself spending too much time making art, and not enough growing your business or fulfilling your professional obligations.

A good solution to the "division of labor" problem is to look at the big picture of your work and decide how much time you can realistically afford to spend on each discipline without harming the other. Then devise a schedule that helps you maintain this balance. You might allocate a certain number of days as sacrosanct "studio time" each week, with the rest of your time devoted to your other work. This isn't foolproof, but it usually produces better results than trying to decide on a day-by-day basis how to spend your time—which makes it more likely you'll take the path of least Resistance.

Another challenge for Symbiotic Creatives is a sense of split identity: this isn't typically as acute as in the Day Jobs and Night Flights model, but it can be disorienting to be an artist or dancer one moment, and a teacher or consultant the next. And success can bring unexpected problems: the better known you become in your primary creative discipline, the more restricted you may feel by your secondary discipline; alternatively, you might achieve great success in your secondary discipline, and realize to your horror that the world now sees you as a teacher, editor, or consultant rather than an artist.

The identity problem can be solved to a certain extent by time management: if you can allocate different days to different roles, it's much easier than continually switching between them throughout the day. Another thing is to take time out to look at the big picture every so often and ask yourself: "*Am I satisfied with my progress in both roles? If one is being neglected, how can I carve out more time for it, or raise my profile in this role?*"

EXEMPLAR: JOANNA PENN, AUTHOR, SPEAKER, ENTREPRENEUR

Joanna Penn is a *New York Times* and *USA Today* bestselling thriller author as J.F.Penn (JFPenn.com), and writes nonfiction for authors as Joanna Penn. She is a professional speaker and award-winning entrepreneur. Her site TheCreativePenn.com is regularly voted one of the Top 10 sites for writers. Connect with Joanna on Twitter @thecreativepenn

Why did you become a novelist? What do you love about writing fiction?

I've always been a reader. My Mum says when I used to come into her room at night as a little girl, I would drag my favorite books, not a teddy. My childhood was spent in libraries and as an introvert, I've always preferred to be alone with a book than in groups. I only recently realized that this personality trait makes writing the ideal life for me.

Like many people, I ended up in a job because of circumstance, and found myself in my thirties wondering what I was doing with my life. I had a four-bedroom house, a good job, and all the trappings of a so-called successful corporate life, but I was miserable. I started reading self-help books, then wrote my first nonfiction book—which changed my life and led me into learning about self-publishing and creative entrepreneurship.

I started a blog and podcast about what I was learning, and then in 2009 I joined NaNoWriMo—National Novel Writing Month—and tried my hand at fiction. The words I wrote that month contained the seed of *Stone of Fire*, my first novel. I caught the writing bug and now I can't write fast enough to capture all the stories in my head.

I love writing fiction because it's so surprising. I look back at my books and wonder where the words came from. Often there will be aspects of my life that I thought were buried and forgotten. I travel for research and I have real-life adventures that emerge in the books.

I also have something tangible to show for my time—and fiction doesn't age. My stories can be read a hundred years from now and there will still be something human that could touch someone in another time. Nonfiction doesn't do that because the world changes so fast, and often nonfiction books become obsolete. But a story is always new to the person who finds it, no matter when it was published. So fiction is amazing on a creative level, but also as a business model. Fiction can earn you money for the rest of your life, and 70 years after you die, according to copyright law. Wow!

What do you love about teaching, podcasting, and writing nonfiction guides for authors? How does this differ from what you love about writing fiction?

Writing fiction is inherently selfish, in that I am in my own head, writing the stories that obsess me. In writing nonfiction, I am always focused on the reader and how I can help them. I think most people have a desire to help, and so writing nonfiction gives me the chance to change lives, especially in a time when creative entrepreneurs are busting myths about long-established industries.

I'm passionate about the rise of independent creators—for example, indie music, indie film, indie authors. It used to be that most people only consumed books, TV, and radio. Now we can write and publish our own books, produce YouTube videos with bigger audiences than mainstream TV, and podcast to millions of listeners from home. It's an exciting time to be a creative!

I also want to prove that the creative path can be a valid career choice. In fact, as the world shifts from big corporates to small entrepreneurial companies, being creative will increasingly be the most important skill. By teaching and podcasting and writing, I hope to spread this creative entrepreneurial movement. So it's a combination of things, but every day I wake up with more to share!

How do your two creative disciplines complement and support each other?

I compare it to Plato's Chariot, where the white and black horses pull the chariot and both are needed to make it run in a straight line. If one horse dominates, the chariot may overturn or head off in the wrong direction.

In our lives, we all have a light and dark side. My "shadow side," as Carl Jung described it, is my fiction. I let the shadow play there, and write what emerges from my subconscious. The light side is my teaching and nonfiction books, the aspects that help more people but perhaps don't feed my soul as much. I need both.

Fiction drains me more in terms of creative exhaustion, and I like to write nonfiction in between books as a kind of palette cleanser, a way to allow the creative well to refill before I write fiction again.

60 per cent of my book income is based on fiction sales, but I also use my nonfiction books for other revenue streams like courses and professional speaking. So I also need both in order to make a good living as a creative.

Is there any conflict between your two disciplines? If so, how do you deal with this?

The conflict comes in managing my time between the two aspects. I feel a constant tension, and several times have considered giving up one or the other. But this is where the adage "Know yourself" applies. My personality has both sides, so my creative life needs to incorporate both as well.

I manage the tension by scheduling my diary by each author name—I have J.F. Penn days when I focus on fiction, and then Joanna Penn days when I do nonfiction, courses, and speaking.

When I'm writing the first draft of a novel I blank out a whole month for J.F. Penn so I can get down into that deeper level of creativity without being disturbed. As Joanna Penn I am much more sociable. But it's definitely a daily battle for me to ensure they are both part of my life.

How and when do you think about extrinsic rewards—such as money, fame, reputation, and opportunity? Does this differ between your two creative roles?

Artists have stomachs, they need to eat! I am a full-time creative entrepreneur so income streams are important for paying the bills. So I think about growing my income most days, as I have no separation between art and business in my conscious mind. But I left a highly paid corporate job to become an author, so clearly money is less important to me than finding meaning in what I do!

However, when I write fiction, my unconscious mind tends to dominate and the extrinsic rewards fall away. For example, a while back I decided to write a mainstream crime novel, a police procedural that would sell well in the UK. But once I started writing what became *Desecration*, the book shifted into something cross-genre, a crime thriller with a supernatural edge. I've found over time that I always write with an edge of the supernatural. That's what fascinates me, so I just have to accept that, even if it is not so commercial. I have to be true to my Muse, although I certainly use marketing principles to get the books to the readers who will enjoy them.

Who are the most important people in your working life? How are you affected by their influences?

I am mainly influenced by books, courses, and podcasts, as I am a constant learner. I don't believe in having one mentor—I think we can all learn different things from different people. I read three to five books a week, a mixture of fiction and non-fiction, and I write notes when I find something I want to use. I listen to five podcasts a week and pick up things from those too.

At the moment, I am finding Tim Ferriss's podcast very influential in terms of learning about excellence in many different industries, as well as habits that help achievement. I'm also reading and listening to everything Peter Diamandis does in terms of what will change in the world in the next 25 years. His book *Abundance* is a great place to start. I am building a long-term business and I'm a bit of a futurist, so I am always interested in what's coming next.

5. Creative Entrepreneurship

Creative Entrepreneurship means taking a creative approach to growing a business—creating and selling artworks, products, and services to people who love your work and believe in your mission.

"Mission?"

That's right. A truly Creative Entrepreneur is motivated by more than money—she wants to change the world, help people, and change their lives in some way. That could mean delighting and challenging them with her artwork, helping them with game-changing products, or providing a service that transforms their life, career, or business.

Superficially, Creative Entrepreneurship looks similar to Lucrative Art but it's not quite the same: a Lucrative Artist likes to earn money, but his main focus is his art, so he may prefer to leave the "business side of things" to others wherever possible. But a Creative Entrepreneur doesn't see such a black-and-white distinction between art and business: she finds the challenge of growing a business inspiring in its own right, and loves to experiment with innovative business models, organizational structures, and approaches to marketing to take the business to new levels.

Some people start their career as artists, go on to become Lucrative Artists, and then develop into Creative Entrepreneurs when they see the potential to grow a business based on their work. Others are entrepreneurs first and foremost: they love the challenge of identifying a market and creating products or services that will delight and/or solve problems for their customers.

Some creatives object to the word "entrepreneur"—to them, it sounds very corporate and uncreative. But if we look at the original French, it means something very simple: from *entreprendre*, "to undertake,"—an entrepreneur is "someone who undertakes." Someone who makes things happen.

PROS

When you start to think and act like a Creative Entrepreneur, you can find ways to earn more money with less time and effort: e.g. creating a piece of art, licensing it to a company, and getting paid over and over for something you created once. Or self-publishing a book, investing in editorial services and cover design, and exploiting associated rights (translations, audiobook versions, movie rights) to earn royalties and licensing income from it for the rest of your life. Or creating a product and automated or delegated systems to deliver it, so that it earns you income while you're busy doing other things.

You can spend the time and money you create doing whatever you want: relaxing and enjoying life; funding other creative projects; making a difference in the world; or simply spending more time on your own creative work.

For a true Creative Entrepreneur, there is no tension between art and business, creativity and money: each supports the other. And you find all of it inspiring in different ways.

As with Symbiotic Creativity, a change can be as good as a rest: when you're stuck on a painting, you can spend the afternoon reviewing your marketing strategy; when you're feeling the pressures of business, time in the studio can be a great release valve.

If you're a freelance Commercial Creative, I'd say you owe it to yourself to investigate the path of Creative Entrepreneurship: even if you're really good at finding and serving clients, if you stay as a freelancer you will always have to find more clients. But by becoming a Creative Entrepreneur you can develop assets and innovate with your business model in ways that can earn you more money for your time and effort as the years go by.

CONS

Becoming an entrepreneur is a big learning curve, and not for the fainthearted. You need to learn new skills, challenge yourself on a daily basis, and be prepared to take risks and deal with the consequences when things go wrong.

If you're a Lucrative Artist making the transition to Creative Entrepreneurship, it's uncomfortable to move from one sphere where you're operating at a high level, to another where you may be a beginner. Whether you succeed depends on how much you relish and commit to the challenge—entrepreneurship is hard, but no harder than making art, so if you *really* want it and you're prepared to learn from feedback and experience, you can do it.

Business, like art, can be all consuming, and some creators decide that the rewards of Creative Entrepreneurship are not worth the sacrifice of time away from their first creative love; they prefer to stay as Lucrative Artists, delegating all the "business stuff" to trusted advisers, and accept the relative loss of control over their business affairs as a price worth paying.

Depending on the nature of your business, you may find it puts you in the public eye or demands that you interact with others in ways you are not comfortable with. If you're a novelist used to sitting at home uploading books to Amazon, you may not relish the prospect of meeting with challenging clients or suppliers and negotiating the terms you want. Even if you're comfortable in front of a live audience as a performer, you may find it challenging to have to deal with unhappy customers or make public statements if your business is attacked. If this applies to you, then you have a choice: either learn to become a better communicator and develop a thicker skin for criticism (which is eminently achievable if you want it), or pick another Creative Career Model.

EXEMPLARS

For this model I have two exemplars—a Commercial Creative-turned-Creative Entrepreneur, James Chartrand; and a Lucrative Artist-turned-Creative Entrepreneur, Natasha Wescoat.

EXEMPLAR 1: JAMES CHARTRAND, COPYWRITER AND ENTREPRENEUR

James Chartrand is an expert copywriter with a decade of experience in the field, and she's (yes, she) the owner of Men with Pens (MenWithPens.ca), a digital marketing agency, and Damn Fine Words (DamnFineWords.com), the game-changing writing course she created for business owners. James loves the color blue, her kids, Nike sneakers, and ice skating, and the rumors about James being a little old-school are true: she still believes that getting to know her readers one-on-one makes for better, more personal connections for greater business success.

How did you get started in business? What made you pick copywriting?

Once upon a time I found myself facing some hard decisions. I had two young daughters to take care of. I was single and alone, having left an unhealthy relationship, and I was living in a crappy, tiny apartment. I'd used up my savings trying to make ends meet, supplementing as best I could with the money I earned from a dangerous part-time job. I had been looking for a better job, but there were none to be had in the low-income/high-unemployment area where I lived.

The welfare application was on my kitchen table. It was filled out and signed, waiting for me to bring it to the people who would decide whether I'd be able to make rent next month or put food on the table. My older daughter told me she could look for work to help pay the bills. She was 12.

As a last-ditch resort, I turned to the internet, thinking there must be something I could do . . . maybe in writing. I was a good writer.

Sure enough, there was writing work for the taking, and payment was quick and easy. It definitely wasn't lucrative at first, but I was grateful for a way to get out of this mess. I spent the first month working hard for next to nothing ($1 for 500 words!) and the next five months building myself a successful copywriting business that earned tens of thousands of dollars. Within a year, I had a stable of 30 writers. Within three, I was considered an expert in the field.

Ten years later my company pulls in six figures each year, has four separate divisions (training, copywriting, website design, and consulting), and is still growing—though my stable of writers has settled down to a small, boutique team of my very best staff.

What aspects of writing and business do you enjoy the most?
What I enjoy most about either changes as I change as a person. Ten years ago, I would've said I enjoyed the respect and attention. Eight years ago, I might've said I enjoyed the freedom of setting my own schedule, or that my career involved playing with words. Five years ago, I might've said I was proud of the fact I became a Canadian corporation.

Today, I enjoy the money. I have a beautiful home, a healthy family, and life is quite good. And I enjoy the fact that if I need $1,000 for whatever reason, I can make that money happen. It's like a choose-your-own adventure book, only it's the story of your life.

But what I really enjoy, beyond the writing, beyond owning a company, beyond even earning good money, is hearing someone say, "Thank you. That made a big difference in my life."

I don't really want to change the world, but knowing I've made someone else's life better really turns my crank. Maybe a local business is struggling, and one small change I suggest turns everything around for them. Maybe a writer I know is stuck, and my advice unblocks the obstacle for her. Whether the result is big or small, seeing that change unfold and watching it create results provides intrinsic value for me—it tells me that my advice really does make a difference, in visible, tangible ways.

What kind of clients do you like to work with the most? Why?

The usual applies: I like people who respect me, my skill levels, and my talents, and who trust me to do my job. (And who pay on time, of course.)

But the people I really enjoy working with are those who could use a break—the underdogs. The ones who are trying so hard to succeed despite all the odds, who really want to win and don't quite believe they can. Those are the people whose lives I can truly change. Those are the ones who, after working with me, almost invariably say, "Thank you. That made a big difference in my life." When that happens, I'm on top of the world because I've done right by those who need it most.

When and how do you think about external factors, such as money, awards, fame, and creative reputation?

Every single day. External factors are crucial to the perception of those who might work with me, so I can't neglect them. People need to know that I operate a successful company with a well-known reputation for quality, because that encourages them to approach me for their own projects.

Plus, on a personal level, it's important for me to be seen as someone successful, with a good creative reputation—I certainly don't want to be known as a struggling artist! And on a practical level, money is important to my creativity. If I'm worrying about how to pay the bills, I don't have a peaceful mind that can focus on writing or come up with ideas.

What made you transition from a service provider to creating and marketing your own courses as an entrepreneur?

I used to receive emails from all sorts of people asking, "James, where can I learn to do what you do?" I knew a lot of these people as friends, and it hurt to have to tell them that I didn't know any resources that would help.

I'd read the books and they weren't helpful. I'd read the blogs and they weren't so great either. I'd seen the very few courses available and they definitely weren't ones I'd recommend. No one could help these people, and no resource was available to them—so I decided to create what they needed.

My motivations were partially selfish, I'll admit. I love helping people, so each time someone asked for my advice, I'd write a long email packed with advice. Then someone else would ask for help, and I'd write them a long email too.

Being generous and kind is a good thing, but not when it takes away from the time you need to earn a living. So I realized that creating a course could solve several problems in one fell swoop:

- I could give people my best advice, providing them with the learning they sought
- I could fulfill my internal need of knowing I've helped others
- I could free up my time for my own projects and client work
- I could earn money from the advice I had been giving away for nothing

- I could hear the "Thanks, that made a difference" when my advice helped others succeed

Seemed like a great deal to me!

I never imagined that my courses would take off and become as popular as they did. At the time, I was just thinking, "What would Darryl need to know? What would be useful to Sarah?" I tried to cover everything that would make a big difference in these people's lives. I wanted to make sure that when people asked me for a recommendation, I could answer, "Here, take this course. It'll help." And it does!

Who are the most important people in your working life, and how do their influences affect you?

One of the most important influences in my business is a good personal connection with my readership. Without them responding, my writing would be an exercise in vanity, without any impact on anyone else's life!

And without that personal connection with my readership, I tend to flounder. What advice should I give? What would help people most? I could throw out random smart advice, but that's useless to everyone. I'd much rather focus on something real, tangible, and specific.

Plus, feedback from my readers helps them provide me with that crucial, "Thanks, James, this helped so much!" that I need to hear to stay motivated to give of myself!

EXEMPLAR 2: NATASHA WESCOAT, ARTIST AND ENTREPRENEUR

Michigan native Natasha Wescoat (Natasha-Wescoat.com) comes from a family of artists. Her work is an enigmatic mix of colors and moving worlds filled with fantasy characters and dreamy landscapes. She is widely known for her iconic *Jeweled Trees*™ which hang in private and corporate collections worldwide and have rocked Hollywood and classrooms alike. Natasha has exhibited nationally in galleries, art fairs, and special events across the USA. Her work has appeared in publications including *Professional Artist Magazine*, and *Artist's & Graphic Designer's Market*. She has licensed her images for use as murals, cards, bags, olive oil bottles, and other products. Natasha is also the author of the children's book, *Charlotte Lively and the Not-So-Wicked Witch*. (CharlotteLively.com)

What made you want to be an artist? What aspects of making art do you enjoy the most?

I've had the determination since I was five. I would ask my grandmother for their Sunday paper to read the comics and suddenly realized my love of drawing had the possibility of being a full time job—that really sparked my interest. Since that year I have been relentless throughout my life in pursuing that dream.

I enjoy the ability to create something that I thought of in my head. There's nothing quite like being able to show someone a vision of your idea on paper. That was exciting in itself. None of the other aspects have been as important or as exciting as the fact that I have the ability to show something in my own mind to someone else without having to describe it.

When and how do you think about external factors, such as money, awards, fame, and artistic reputation?

I started focusing on this when I was very young. It was after I discovered that art could be a job that I started striving and working hard to make something of my work.

I practiced every single day. Starting at age nine, I mailed people at Disney animation studios, Oprah, and places I found through *Cartoon Saturdays* (a weekly TV program)—to share my art with anyone I could get to put their eyeballs on the work. I participated in contests, searching the event walls of my high school, asking my teachers and looking through magazines. If I found something on my own, I would sign up and participate right away. If the teacher offered the option, I took it. I asked for extra credit in art classes to improve my skills.

I was an abnormal child when it came to this. I really took it seriously, without any pressure from my parents to do it.

These days I'm motivated more by the financial aspects than I'd ever be about fame or artistic reputation. I care very little about recognition, and never have been interested in what people think about me as an artist or how big I would ever get. It was always about how this could provide a living for me, and I'm sure this might be a turn off to some artists, but I really think more about this as a form of work than as something to express myself. I love making art, but I don't have the luxury of treating this as a pure passion project. It's one of the only marketable skills I have as a responsible adult, and has always been the only option for work.

You're very creative at finding new markets for your work, e.g. exhibiting your art in hotels as well as galleries, and licensing your images for use in products. Do you enjoy this

entrepreneurial creativity? How different is it to your artistic creativity?

In many ways I definitely do. And this is something I love teaching other artists who might not have the natural inclination towards it that I do. Entrepreneurship, marketing, and relationship marketing are as creative as the art itself.

I used to be a heavy gamer up until I was 21, so when I started my art business, I began to "gamify" the whole business/career building process. It made every day really exciting to get up and keep hustling and working for new opportunities.

There is a side to it that is much more logical and analytical than the art creating, definitely. I find that I am much more analytical than anything else in my personality, but I'm also very quick in that I can see the big picture of an idea in a few minutes and know what the strategy is to lay out.

Entrepreneurship is a lot like a game of war, but one without the other is death to me—I need art as much as I need the game of business.

Who are the most important people in your working life, and how do their influences affect you?

Unfortunately I don't have that, as I have worked by myself for the last 12 years. That can be draining and depressing at times. I need to be surrounded by other people, as I've previously been in very socially-based work as a former minister. I like working with others and collaborating as well as that ability to be a mentor. It's vital for every human being to have that kind of interaction, not only for the support but for keeping things in perspective, growing on a personal level, creative level, and business level. You cannot work alone all the time. I've had experience in working with others when it came to my marketing projects, or at one time my live painting events, and that has been a wonderful and inspiring experience. It helped me keep things in perspective and to realize my potential.

Mixing models

You've probably noticed there are overlaps among different Creative Career Models. Just as a business can have several business models for different product lines and services, so you can make use of two or more Creative Career Models at different stages of your career, or even simultaneously.

My poetry and creative coaching are forms of Symbiotic Creativity: the poetry is something I do for love. It also confronts me with many of the creative challenges my clients face. The coaching is inspiring and challenging in its own right, and it also supports me and my poetry.

My coaching, books for creatives (like this one), and training programs can also be seen as forms of Commercial Creativity. And I certainly consider myself a Creative Entrepreneur—over the years I've experimented with many different ways of working, business models, products and services, online and offline, digital and physical, working one-to-one and with groups, in order to find the right balance for me and create the most value for my readers, customers, and clients. Similarly, I could have placed several of my Exemplars in more than one category. All of them are Creative Entrepreneurs to some degree.

Think of the four basic types of motivation as primary colors in your motivational palette—you can mix them in different combinations to paint your Creative Motivation Pinwheel. The five Creative Career Models illustrate some of the patterns you can create. Making your pinwheel, painting it, and getting it to spin is a messy, experimental process. Some days it feels like you have to huff and puff to get it to turn even a little. But all the effort is worthwhile on the days when your inspiration, ambition, desires, and influences are aligned—days when the pinwheel spins effortlessly, caught by a bigger breeze.

NEXT STEPS

A free course for you

Over 10,000 people have taken my free 26-week creative career course, The Creative Pathfinder.

The course covers the whole range of skills you need to succeed as a 21st-century creative professional, including:

- creative thinking
- productivity for creatives
- growing your network
- promoting your work
- selling without selling your soul
- managing money
- dealing with rejection and criticism
- making the most of your intellectual property
- creative presentation skills

Creative Pathfinder students are also the first to know when I release a new book (usually at a substantial discount).

Enroll on the course at: LateralAction.com/Pathfinder

Your opinion counts

Thank you for reading this far—I hope you found the book helpful and I wish you success and fulfillment on your journey.

I'd appreciate it if you would take a few moments to leave a brief review of *Motivation for Creative People*. As well as helping me, it will help other creatives decide whether the book is for them.

For your convenience this page links to all the online stores where the book is available: LateralAction.com/Motivation

Beyond motivation . . . Resilience

If you want to achieve something original and meaningful with your life, you *must* learn to deal with rejection and criticism.

If you're an artist of any kind your work will be rejected by editors, curators, and other gatekeepers. Each time you put it in front of the public, you expose yourself to criticism.

If you're a freelancer or entrepreneur you face rejection by (potential) customers, partners, and investors. Those same people won't hesitate to criticize you if they are unhappy.

If you're chasing your dream job you'll receive your share of rejection letters. And once you land the job, taking flak when things go wrong is part of the deal.

Many people set out on their chosen path full of hope and inspiration, only to turn back because they can't deal with the emotional impact of crushing rejections and vicious criticism.

In *Resilience: Facing Down Rejection and Criticism on the Road to Success*, I explain why your reactions to rejection and criticism are completely normal—and how to deal with them effectively.

Through stories from my own experience as well as those of famous creators, I will show you that you are far from alone in suffering from rejection and criticism.

Like *Motivation for Creative People*, *Resilience* is based on my experience of coaching hundreds of creative people like you, so the ideas are tried-and-tested.

You will discover:

- Why rejection and criticism hurt so much
- Several ways you may be making rejection worse (without realizing it)
- How to keep going in the face of multiple rejections
- Why your Inner Critic is (potentially) your best friend

- When to ignore the critics—and when to listen
- Whether (and how) to respond to insults and abuse
- Why success is harder than it looks—and how to deal with it

This is not a theoretical book—it's packed with practical tips and techniques you can apply to your own challenges right away.

Whether you're just setting out, in the middle of your journey, or dealing with the unexpected challenges of success, *Resilience* will show you how to keep moving forward.

Pick up a copy of *Resilience* at: LateralAction.com/Resilience

"Read this book and you will be bulletproof!"

| Steven Pressfield, bestselling author of *The War of Art* and *Turning Pro*

Coaching with Mark

I coach creative professionals who want to achieve great things with their lives.

They are drawn from the entire spectrum of the creative industries: fine artists, entertainers, commercial creatives, and creative entrepreneurs.

They live all over the world—the internet means I can coach them wherever they are.

They are doing work they—and I—find inspiring.

They are ambitious to succeed professionally as well as creatively.

Learn more about my coaching: LateralAction.com/Coaching

To leaders of creative teams

Motivation for Creative People is a revised and expanded version of a blog series and ebook I wrote in 2008, called *How to Motivate Creative People (Including Yourself)*.

The initial impetus came from a question from a manager about how to motivate his staff when salaries had frozen and bonuses had vanished in the wake of the financial crash. I wanted to show managers of creative teams that the traditional "carrot and stick" approach to management is likely to backfire when used with creative workers. The book shows how to motivate creative employees by tapping into the powerful inner drive creative professionals bring to work every day.

If you are a leader or manager challenged with getting the best out of creative workers, and you would like a copy of my original ebook *How to Motivate Creative People (Including Yourself)*, email me at Mark@LateralAction.com and I will send it to you with my compliments.

About the author

Mark McGuinness is a poet and coach who has been helping creative professionals since 1996.

His poems are published in leading poetry journals, and he writes about classic and contemporary poetry at: MarkMcGuinness.com

Mark's first book *Resilience: Facing Down Rejection and Criticism on the Road to Success* is an Amazon Creativity bestseller. He is also a co-author of the bestsellers *Manage Your Day-to-Day* and *Maximize Your Potential*, both published by 99U.

Based in the UK, Mark coaches clients all over the world via the magic of the internet. He also consults for leading creative agencies and studios. His blog at LateralAction.com is read by thousands of people every week, and over 10,000 students have taken his free course The Creative Pathfinder.

His work has been featured in publications including *Creative Review*, the *Wall Street Journal,* and *Vogue US*, and on television at the Discovery Health Channel.

Contact Mark: Mark@LateralAction.com
Coaching enquiries: LateralAction.com/Coaching
Twitter: @markmcguinness
Facebook: Facebook.com/LateralAction

Thank you

To my clients and readers, unfailing sources of social motivation.

To Johan Adda, Scott Belsky, Aileen Bennett, James Chartrand, Theo Lipfert, CJ Lyons, Joanna Penn, Steven Pressfield, Scott Purnell, Natasha Wescoat, and Josh Zepps, for enriching the book with their contributions.

To Irene Hoffman, for the pinwheel metaphor and designing a beautiful and usable book.

To David Colin Carr, for editing the book and guiding me through the wilds of US usage.

To Jarie Bolander, Kerri Ho, Melanie Pryor, and Aileen Tu, for reading the manuscript and giving me valuable feedback.

To Sarah Ridley, for meticulous proofreading.

To Polgarus Studio, for formatting the ebook edition.

To James Chartrand, for help with the book description.

To Chris Bilton and Ruth Leary of the MA in Creative and Media Enterprises at Warwick University, for introducing me to the research on motivation and creativity, and for stimulating discussions that helped me develop my ideas.

To Steven Pressfield, for inspiration and example.

To Scott Belsky, Sean Blanda, Sasha VanHoven, and the rest of the team at Behance, for inviting me to be part of their tribe at the 99U Conference and online at 99U.com

To Jocelyn Glei, my former editor at 99U, for steering me towards clarity.

To Mimi Khalvati, for making excellence so appealing.

To Peleg Top, for reminding me of what's truly important. (And booking the Kate Bush tickets!)

To Rich Litvin and Steve Chandler, for challenging me to be a better coach.

To Mum and Dad, for encouraging me from the start.

Made in the USA
Middletown, DE
30 October 2019